The devotions in this collection are fil. ...gn-ancy, and hey-girlfriend-I've-been-there wisdom that will touch all women on some level. What a delightful way to be reminded of God's grace!

Debby Mayne, author of *Sweet Baklava*
and the Class Reunion series

Heartwarming and encouraging, this devotional will refresh your spirit and inspire you to new heights. If you're short on time but yearn for meaningful truths to start your day, this is the book for you.

Diann Hunt, author of *Love Letters in the Sand*

These authors have just the right blend of sass and sanctity. Each devo will be an extra shot of blessing to readers!

Andrea Boeshaar, author of the acclaimed
Seasons of Redemption series

Grace is the most marvelous and mysterious of God's gifts, and these wonderful writers give us fresh, relevant insights on this oldest and most treasured theme of undeserved favor. A wonderful way to begin the day—or end it.

Susan Meissner, author of *Lady in Waiting*

Care for a double shot of espresso? Why not make that a quadruple? These four ladies have perked up a rich, fragrant brew full to the brim with a generous serving of God's grace. With transparency and honesty, the authors open their lives and invite us in for a time of fellowship and spiritual refreshment. This is the perfect devotional for those seeking an inspiring pick-me-up.

Virginia Smith, award-winning author of
A Daughter's Legacy and Lost Melody (with Lori Copeland)

I was moved by every devotion! These women gathered their hearts and courage, poured them onto the page, and trumpeted that our God brings victory over all trials and pain. I loved this collection.

Rachel Hauck, award-winning,
best-selling author of *Dining with Joy*

These are devotions that bring the words of the Bible into the twenty-first century and illustrate how God is the same today as He always was…and will be. I know these four women, and they walk the talk. These daily messages will bless your day.

Lena Nelson Dooley, award-winning author of *Love Finds You in Golden, New Mexico*, and the McKenna's Daughters series

With both humor and poignancy, the devotions will draw you into the writers' lives like they're old friends, and they will also draw your heart into the Father's arms. This is a wonderful collection that will jump-start your day like a good cup o' joe.

Camy Tang, author of *Protection for Hire* and *Stalker in the Shadow*s and contributor to the Patchwork Mysteries series

This collection of daily readings packs a jolt of grace that reminds the reader that God doesn't skimp when he fills our cups to running over. The authors are transparent about their own need for God's abundant, never-decaffeinated grace, and their stories invite others to sip the same fully-loaded delight.

Michelle Rayburn, writer, speaker, and daughter of an ovarian cancer survivor

Full-strength—that describes their coffee and their God. With loads of wit and hard-won wisdom, these women serve up hope with an extra shot of joy. You will laugh out loud and go through your day knowing that, even when you feel weak, your God is "strong enough."

Kathi Lipp, speaker and author of *The Husband Project*

Grab a cup of your favorite java and join the authors for a few moments of girl talk about the most amazing thing in the universe—God's grace. Their stories will touch your heart, lighten your load, and give you a quadruple shot of encouragement for your day!

Gwen Ford Faulkenberry, author of *Love Finds You in Branson, Missouri*

This devotional should be labeled "Manual for Life." The authors show the pains, problems, and persisting nightmares of everyday life and balance them with the light of hope in Jesus. I definitely recommend this devotional for anyone seeking to find God's assurance and encouragement.

Tracie Peterson, best-selling author of *Striking a Match*, *Song of Alaska*, and the Heirs of Montana series

What do you get when you merge four of my favorite authors, a cup of coffee, and a grace-filled message? One of the best devotionals for women in recent years. This devotional invigorates the soul in much the same way that your morning cup o' joe invigorates the body. Highly recommended.

Janice Hanna Thompson, author of *Hello, Hollywood!*

This is the perfect blend of voices, hearts, experiences, and honest confessions from four well-known authors to women just like us. Sandie, Loree, Trish, and Cynthia have all walked in our shoes…and lived to tell about it. Better yet, they didn't just survive the bumps and nuclear explosions of life, they grew and blossomed in the middle of them. And now they've teamed up to offer the rest of us a "word in season" to encourage, uplift, strengthen, and bless us right when we need it most. A practical, pithy, and poignant collection of devotionals from sisters who care!

Kathi Macias, author of the best-selling women's devotional *A Moment a Day*

This is a powerful compilation of encouragement and reminders of how big our God truly is, and that His grace is indeed more than we could ever need or want. The authors brought me to tears and laughter and—even better—challenged me in my daily walk with the Lord. Beautifully and simply written, this book is one to cherish and pass on to many.

Kimberley Woodhouse, author of *Welcome Home: Our Family's Journey to Extreme Joy*, *No Safe Haven*, and *Race Against Time*

GRACE
is like
chocolate
without the
calories

GRACE
is like
chocolate
without the
calories

DEVOTIONS ABOUT GOD'S GOODNESS

BRICKER | LOUGH | PERRY | RUCHTI

WORTHY®
Inspired

Published by Worthy Inspired, an imprint of Worthy Publishing Group, a division of Worthy Media, Inc., One Franklin Park, 6100 Tower Circle, Suite 210, Franklin, TN 37067.

WORTHY is a registered trademark of Worthy Media, Inc.

HELPING PEOPLE EXPERIENCE THE HEART OF GOD

eBook available wherever digital books are sold.

Library of Congress Cataloging-in-Publication Data

Names: Bricker, Sandra D., 1958- author.
Title: Grace is like chocolate without the calories : devotions about God's
    goodness / by Sandra D. Bricker, Loree Lough, Trish Perry, and Cynthia
    Ruchti.
Description: Franklin, TN : Worthy Publishing, 2017.
Identifiers: LCCN 2017005514 | ISBN 9781683970330 (tradepaper)
Subjects: LCSH: Christian life--Meditations. | Christian life--Anecdotes. |
    Prayers.
Classification: LCC BV4501.3 .B7477 2017 | DDC 242/.2--dc23
LC record available at https://lccn.loc.gov/2017005514

Unless otherwise noted all Scripture references are from the Holy Bible, New International Version®, NIV®. Copyright © 1973, 1978, 1984, 2011 by Biblica, Inc.® All rights reserved worldwide. | Scripture quotations marked KJV are taken from the King James Version of the Bible. | Scripture references marked NKJV are from the Holy Bible, New King James Version®. Copyright © 1982 by Thomas Nelson, Inc. Used by permission.

ISBN: 978-1-68397-033-0

Cover Design: Melissa Reagan

Printed in the United States of America

17 18 19 20 21 22 LBM 10 9 8 7 6 5 4 3 2 1

*Grace, mercy and peace from God the Father
and from Jesus Christ, the Father's Son,
will be with us in truth and love.*

2 JOHN 1:3

Foreword

It's not uncommon to hear Sandie Bricker's friends say that they felt like sisters with Sandie within minutes of meeting her. She had that quality about her, that welcoming warmth that made a hug much more practical and desired than a mere handshake. But beyond that, it was shortly into conversation with Sandie that it became obvious she cared deeply about the heart need of the person with whom she conversed. All of us authors in this volume experienced that personally. Which is part of why we feel her absence from this earth so keenly now that she has departed its gravity for the freedom and joy of heaven with her Savior.

Dedicating this book of devotional thoughts to her is fitting for so many reasons. Her gratitude for God's overflowing grace shown brightly—blingingly—in her life, on her face, and in her relationships. Her exuberance for the life-changing topic spilled over onto us as we wrote, and onto anyone who came within reach of her influence.

Writer, worshiper, warrior—like King David of the Bible—Sandie leaves a legacy of grace that sweetens every memory we cherish, and a standard to which we aspire. Thank you, dear friend. We'll miss you every day until we see you again.

Loree Lough, Trish Perry, & Cynthia Ruchti

Introduction

GRACE: noun—*a manifestation of favor or good will; mercy; clemency; pardon; favor shown in granting a delay or temporary immunity.* verb—*a pure, ongoing act of God alone.*

God's grace does what nothing else can. It leaps tall mountains with a single promise: "My grace is sufficient for you, for my power is made perfect in weakness" (2 Corinthians 12:9).

Grace enables us to do the impossible. When we don't have the ability, the resources, or even the drive to accomplish God's will for our lives, His grace is there. And when our feet slip or we've chosen the wrong path, His grace is a heartbeat away to dust us off and show us the way home, no questions asked.

Each one of us has lived with imperfect (perhaps very conditional) love, and the concept of God's perfect love often seems unfathomable by comparison. Complete pardon? Clemency? *Unearned favor?* Oh, come on. What's the catch? Can it really be that, as we navigate the high-wire act of our busy lives, God's grace forms a quiet safety net beneath us?

All those things we turn toward with the hope that they will justify or fortify us in some way—good works, career or family focus, even chocolate or caffeine!—contribute nothing long-lasting. They're just momentary, while the supply of God's grace never runs dry.

So does that mean when you step into line to order your next double espresso, we would suggest that you make it a decaf? *Absolutely not!* But we're here to show you…to gently remind you…that there is nothing else that offers the high-octane surge of His full-on grace.

And the beautiful part? Grace is at its best when you're at your worst. It's one of those mysterious and wonderful promises that He fulfills time and again, whether we understand it or not.

Sandie, Loree, Trish, & Cynthia

Earning Grace...and Other Horror Stories

Out of his fullness we have all received grace in place
of grace already given. For the law was given through Moses;
grace and truth came through Jesus Christ.

JOHN 1:16–17

I'm one of those people who remembers dreams, and usually in great detail. For many years I've tried to figure out what messages my dreams might have for me in hopes that God will use them to communicate with me, like He did with certain men and women of the Bible. Unfortunately, years of dark hallways, growling giraffes, automobile-producing gardens, and missed social studies tests have blown by, unanalyzed, without any deciphered meaning. But the other morning I woke up with a throbbing back after dreaming that I'd been forced to carry my past sins in heavy wineskins over a rocky mountain range. It wasn't too hard to figure out the "hidden message" there as I wobbled toward the beautiful, blue lake where I was allowed to deposit them. I remember thinking, that I felt like one of the contestants on *The Biggest Loser.*

I love that show—partly because I've been fighting the weight battle for my whole life, but also because the brave participants inspire me. Late in each season, the producers set up a challenge for the contestants involving a race where they carry their old weight on their backs. For instance, if one of them has lost a total of 120 pounds, 120 pounds' worth of weighted packs are piled on them in the increments in which they lost it. At intervals throughout the course, they get to drop the packs in the order in which they lost the weight over the weeks.

Every time those incredible shrinking bodies add on the weight they'd been carrying through their lives before arriving at the Biggest Loser campus, I shrink into the sofa and cringe. How horrible! But as they move along the course and drop the first week's loss of twelve pounds, the second week's ten, and so on, viewers can't miss the change in their countenance.

What if we were forced to carry our sins around that way? What if our offenses and mistakes stayed with us in big weighted packs and we had to earn the right to drop them, one by one? What if the forgiveness of sin had to be bought, perhaps by racing, others on a course and competing for forgiveness?

The fullness of God's grace is astounding, isn't it? We don't have to carry those sins on our backs, groaning beneath the weight of them until we've been punished enough, earned enough "grace points," or made a strong enough case for probation. Instead, with one act of utterly unselfish love, we were cleared of all charges. Punishment? Not necessary. Jesus tells us, "I've got this," as He has already taken the beatings and condemnation and shed all the blood on our behalf, leaving behind a steady supply of clean and shiny grace for whenever we need it. ⌒ Sandie

TODAY'S PRAYER
. . . .

Glory, honor, and praise to You, Lord Jesus! I can hardly fathom
the courage and love it took for You to walk away from
Your throne beside the Father in order to take my place,
to shed the blood that would forgive my sins.
I'm humbled and grateful beyond words.

Lone Wolf

He is my loving God and my fortress, my stronghold and my deliverer,
my shield, in whom I take refuge, who subdues peoples under me.

PSALM 144:2

I'm crazy about wolves.

My favorite sanctuary spans acres of tree-lined hills, where nearly fifty wolves, rescued from abuse and neglect, were brought to live with as much dignity as can be achieved in such a scenario.

Five packs live there, and each is led by a strong, capable Alpha pair. They keep order and demand obedience even while at play. You'd think my first stop during visits would be the cubs, but although they're cuter than the Gerber baby, it's the lone wolves that lure me closest.

If you've ever owned a dog, you know that their faces can express joy, fear, and disappointment; I've seen the lone wolves express sadness as they pace the outskirts of pack activity. They understand what we humans can't: they will never be invited into the family circle.

They know, too, that meals will consist of what's left after the others' bellies are full. They're forced to dash in and steal biscuit crumbs, and the crumbs of human affection doled out by caretakers had better be stolen too…if they don't want to pay a painful price. Loners are not allowed to participate in the fun of rowdy rough-housing. They're forbidden from nestling for warmth on cold, dark nights and from cuddling close for comfort when thunder and lightning crash around them.

Even a powerful animal like the wolf can take only so much rejection, and before long, the loners skulk into the forest, starved for food and companionship. And as much as my heart aches for a pack's lone wolves, it's even harder to think of lone wolves of the wilderness, who will never know the kindness and care of human hands.

I think that sometimes we feel a little bit like the sanctuary's lone wolves. When we've suffered the death of a loved one, gone through a divorce, or experienced a job loss, we feel separate and apart from friends and family. Just as the wolves don't trust their own kind, we erroneously convince ourselves that no one can possibly understand what we're going through, and so we skulk off to a forest of our own making: work, alcohol or drugs, the Internet or television. We hide from our spouses, neglect our children, stop walking the dog. We no longer feel like doing good deeds, because we've lost heart.

The wolves don't know to ask God for help. *But we do!*

If only we'd remember that in times of our greatest need, we are cradled in His loving hands, and although we didn't do a thing to earn His tender, merciful care, it's there for the taking.

He has promised that we never need to live on the outskirts, alone and afraid, hungry for compassion and love. Isn't that a miracle? Isn't that a blessing! ∽ Loree

TODAY'S PRAYER

O Lord, I will trust You no matter how dark the nights
or how stormy the seas of my life. When I'm down, lift me up;
when I'm blind to Your grace, open my eyes.
When I'm deaf to the music of Your Word, open my ears.
Though I don't deserve Your loving care, I thank You for it!

I Just Can't
Cut It Alone, Lord

Create in me a pure heart, O God,
and renew a steadfast spirit within me.

PSALM 51:10

Today's verse brings to mind a memory from grade school that is as vivid as if it happened yesterday, which is very weird, considering how insignificant it is. The teacher asked two other girls and me to cut out shapes from construction paper for an upcoming class event. I don't remember the event or even the shape we were creating, but it involved cutting straight lines.

It didn't take more than an effort or two for me to realize that my straight lines were hurting in a big way compared to those of my cohorts. And then the teacher helpfully pointed it out. "Try to be more careful on the rest of them and get them straighter," she said.

Honestly, I tried. I'm sure the tip of my tongue protruded from my pursed lips and my brows furrowed in concentration while I cut my next shape. But it turns out I was straight-line challenged.

And like King David, the author of Psalm 51, I remain straight-line challenged to this day. David wrote this psalm after the prophet Nathan convicted him of his involvement with Bathsheba and his nasty little front-lines setup to get rid of her cuckolded husband. I don't struggle with adultery or murder, but I have yet to go to bed at night knowing I've made it through the day without going outside the lines of who God created me to be.

Yes, I know, as a follower of Christ, I'm a new creation in the eyes of God. Thanks to Christ's standing in for me and paying the price for my sins, God accepts me as clean and blameless—all ready for stepping into heaven at a moment's notice.

But what about today, here on earth, from the moment I spaz awake at the alarm clock to the moment I doze off in bed, praying and occasionally apologizing to the Lord for however I botched up the whole "representing Christ" thing that day? God may consider my *eternal* heart clean, but today? How can my heart be clean if I'm rolling around in envy, anger, impatience, gossip, selfishness, and unwholesome thoughts and words? I may be saved, but I never make it through the day without sinning. I'm not losing my salvation with my daily behavior, but neither am I winning souls to Christ or even living life as fully as He would love for me to live it.

Could get mighty depressing if not for verses like today's. If David did what he did and then stopped to consider how far outside the lines he had strayed and fell humbly to his spiritual knees, pleading, "Create in me a pure heart, O God, and renew a steadfast spirit within me," I suppose that option remains open to me too. Even if I think I've been Miss Perfect Christian today, this prayer should make the cut.

⁓ Trish

TODAY'S PRAYER
. . . .

Gracious Father, Your love and acceptance are amazing,
and I turn continually to You to remember how much
You love me. Thank You for seeing my heart as pure.
Thank You for renewing an unwavering spirit in me,
over and over again.

What the Rain Left

Let my teaching fall like rain and my words descend like dew,
like showers on new grass, like abundant rain on tender plants.
DEUTERONOMY 32:2

When the warm rain cleared that summer afternoon, the grandkids and I dodged (for the most part) the puddles in the driveway as we crossed to the damp but freshly washed grass. The yard had corners yet unexplored, adventures to discover. At four and three, the boys were harder to herd than balls of mercury. My Grammie eyes darted to the dangers—barbed-wire fence, pond, traffic on the county road, poison ivy in the ditch, cockleburs and thistles at the edge of the woods... But their inquisitive gazes, following their big sister, landed on a miniscule movement among the decorative rocks near the house.

Toady frogs.

The kids named them that. Frog-shaped but toad-colored and smaller than the average peanut M&M, the toady frogs held their convention in our yard that day. There were hundreds of them. I had a brief thought about Pharaoh and plagues, but these little gems of creation caused hours of pleasure rather than distress.

Fast but kid-friendly, the toady frogs tolerated capture and investigation by sweaty kid palms. Perfectly camouflaged, they hid among the stones in the landscaping. Squatting like pro golfers lining up a putt, we stared at the rocks until we saw something hop. One-inch toady frogs don't hop far, but the grandchildren's rapt attention registered the motion and sent them scurrying after with cupped hands.

The kids knew capture was temporary. As their for-the-moment science teacher, I explained about how delicately they need to be handled, what toads need to survive, about keeping the noise level low and respecting how God made them and how He wants us to be careful of all the amazing creatures He made. You can't learn about toady frogs without seeing them up close. But, they belong in their own environment, not in a glove.

A glove. That's right. While I scoured the outdoor toys and garden shed for a suitable temporary toad haven, one of the boys found his own creative answer. A translucent garden glove. He found he could fit four or five of the miniature amphibians in each finger. Like dorm rooms centered around a palm-sized main lounge.

There's something about a four-year-old carefully tending a toad-filled glove then gently setting each toad free that makes me smile.

It must have been the warm, tender rain that brought the toads in such numbers. I pray my impromptu science lesson fell like gentle rain too, since that's often how the Lord sends His lessons to my heart.

Like a hand on my shoulder saying, "Hold that more tenderly. You can't keep that forever, you know; we'll have to set it free. Here, let Me show you something amazing about what you've just found."

Sometimes the Lord has to yank me back from the edge of danger. But I'm grateful He also kneels beside me to show me His wonders and whisper His lessons with the tenderness of dew on new grass.
～ Cynthia

TODAY'S PRAYER

Oh, Creator God, what a fascinating world You've made!
Thank You for so often gentling me through
the lessons I need to learn about it.
Fill the gloves of my life with Your delights.

Words: Friend or Foe?

You are the most excellent of men and your lips have been anointed with grace, since God has blessed you forever.

PSALM 45:2

I've always loved words. Reading them, speaking them, hearing them...I just love the language. A creative turn of phrase can stop me in my proverbial tracks, and I consistently strive to string words together in unexpected ways for the greatest impact. Since words are so important to me, you may ask yourself how in the world I recently found myself drowning in an attempt to take a few of them back for tailoring!

A friend who knows that I used to collect vintage jewelry often sends me a box of pieces she's picked up at flea markets or consignment shops. Some of them knock me out, others not so much—the latter of which, I usually put aside to give away. My best girlfriend and I had planned to meet at a conference I was set to attend in Indianapolis, and I wanted something very special for her birthday that same week. When I couldn't find anything just right after a dedicated search, I decided to have a look at my stash of vintage pieces. There was a stunning butterfly necklace in a clean white box that just jumped right out at me. I immediately thought of Marian, and I slipped it into my suitcase on my way to see her.

With very pretty and heartfelt words, I told my friend what she meant to me and how exceptional and special she is, closing with, "I saw this and immediately thought of you!" When she opened the box and saw the necklace, her flawless face dropped like a stone in a clear, still lake. "I'll bet," she replied.

It turned out that the butterfly necklace reminded me of Marian for a very good reason. It hadn't come in a box with a dozen other pieces. In fact, it had been one of several other gifts *Marian had given me* for my own birthday just a few months prior. Apparently it had been a very snug fit around my throat, and I'd placed it with the other pieces to give away. When the memory finally came back to me, my apologies seemed hollow. And I think I was more disappointed than Marian.

We didn't speak of the necklace again during our trip, but amid a later phone conversation I attempted to tell her how sorry I was. The more I tried to explain it, the worse it sounded, even to me.

However, here's the best thing about friends you've known forever: they tend to give you grace. Even though I'd obviously disappointed her, she extended the grace of understanding. In fact, when she flew in to celebrate my birthday this year and gave me several gifts, I told her, "Hey, I have something for you too. It's this beautiful butterfly necklace." And the two of us were—thank the Lord!—able to have a good laugh over it. ⌐ Sandie

TODAY'S PRAYER
. . . .

Thank You, Jesus, for the promise that our lips are anointed
with grace. Even when we say the wrong thing,
You're there to apply the balm.

Muddy Shoes and the Bagel Boys

For the grace of God has appeared that offers salvation to all people.
It teaches us to say "No" to ungodliness and worldly passions,
and to live self-controlled, upright and godly lives in this present age.

TITUS 2:11-12

My gal pals and I were chatting at a corner table in the bagel shop when a well-dressed young fellow walked up to the cashier. Not particularly handsome, he was soft-spoken, polite, and looked shipshape in his polished loafers, silk tie, and crisp white shirt.

"That reminds me," Chrissy said, "of the tie I bought John for our last anniversary…that he never wears."

"And it reminds *me*," groaned Joy, "that since Pete went on a diet, he needs new clothes."

The next man in line left a trail of mud from the door to the counter and then barked out his order so loudly that the people way in back probably heard it too. As I waited to see which of my friends would comment on his rude behavior, Louise piped up with, "For two cents, I'd ask if he's single. He'd be *perfect* for my youngest daughter!"

Back home, I couldn't help but wonder why Louise hadn't seen the quieter, more courteous man as potential son-in-law material, instead of the handsome, inconsiderate one. *So much for that "clothes make the man" rule,* I thought.

Which sparked an idea for my next Sunday school lesson: I'd tell the bagel boys' story exactly as it had happened, with the good-looking loudmouth tracking in mud and the not-so-pretty fellow behaving like a gentleman.

Next, I'd run down the list memorized in business school: Shake hands with confidence. Dress with respect for yourself *and* those around you. Think before you speak, and then speak softly. Stand tall and sit up straight, so your demeanor sends the message that you are a person of good character.

Then I'd back it all up with Scripture references—John 13:34–35 and 1 Corinthians 1:10—and hand out a questionnaire, to make them *think:*

What do you want others to think of you?

What do you want other *Christians* to think of you?

What do *you* think of you?

Have you missed out on a friendship because you judged someone's outward appearance or the way they behaved during that very first meeting?

I'd remind my students of how 1 Samuel 16:7 says that human beings look at what's on the outside, but God looks at our hearts. If we take care of the inside, the outside will take care of itself.

That gave me pause *and* second thoughts because, unless I wanted to teach the kids that I'm a self-righteous jerk, I'd better admit how often I forget it's by God's grace that I have faith. Oh, I'll teach the lesson…someday. In the meantime, the next time I see someone like the handsome loudmouth, I won't judge him ill-bred for not taking off his cap or wiping his feet. — Loree

TODAY'S PRAYER

Dear Lord, open my heart and my eyes too, that I might see
all of Your children with the eyes of blessed grace,
the way You do. In Your most holy name, I pray.

Nocturnal Freak-Out

"So do not fear, for I am with you; do not be dismayed,
for I am your God. I will strengthen you and help you;
I will uphold you with my righteous right hand."

ISAIAH 41:10

The only full-night's sleep I've had recently was when I was under anesthesia for an appendectomy. Apparently, that's what a middle-aged woman has to do to get a proper rest—I say this because I've talked with every woman I know about female sleep issues.

As a child, I enjoyed the slumber of the innocent, the clueless, the pampered. When I got married and had children of my own, that fell apart. Newborns needed feeding, toddlers needed dry sheets, and teens needed to remember curfews so Mom could relax once her offspring were safe at home.

After my teenagers became responsible adults, I graduated to a new phase in life. I started to experience a little thing I like to call "nocturnal freak-out." I know it's all tied to the lovely changes a woman's body goes through as she ages, but that knowledge doesn't help at three o'clock in the morning. I don't need to have a crisis in my life. I simply awaken to answer nature's call.

And then, regardless of how hard I try to remain groggy, it's as if someone pulled the ignition cord on my brain's lawn mower. My neurons become heat-seeking missiles, determined to find a target to stress about. Within seconds of awakening, I latch onto a number of issues that absolutely must be solved before I can sleep again. Will the sale of my daughter's house go through? Will my son get his term paper turned in on time? Was that little noise my microwave made something I need to address? Did I gain weight from that decadent chocolate cake last night? Did I forget to compliment last night's hostess about her awesome chocolate cake? Will I meet my book deadline? How is my heroine going to solve the problem I threw at her yesterday? Why is my hair falling out? Why didn't I work out yesterday?

You get the picture.

I don't claim to have found a miracle cure for this kind of freak-out, whether it happens in the middle of the night or smack in the middle of the day. But recently the Lord did see fit to bless me with today's verse, and I'm telling you, its effects are immediate. I just have to remember its promise.

I haven't read commentaries on this verse. I haven't studied it in any devotional. But it has become my refuge in times of worry. It has settled in my mind to combat my nocturnal freak-outs. I like to think that God was referring to Jesus when He mentioned His "righteous right hand." God will uphold me through His righteous Right Hand. My Savior. Jesus.

No matter what worries whir in my mind in the middle of the night or in the bustle of the day, with that kind of promise, I know it's all going to work out. ⸻ Trish

TODAY'S PRAYER

Precious Lord God, You are my sovereign King, and You know
how easily I fall into worrying, even when I'm half asleep.
Thank You for showing me this verse and for the promise
You made to Your people years and years ago.

Necklace of Contrasts

*Let the one who is wise heed these things
and ponder the loving deeds of the LORD.*

PSALM 107:43

Something's wrong if my jewelry can move seamlessly from my bedroom to the grandkids' dress-up box. I admit, most of my jewelry comes from clearance racks. The good news is that none of it has to be insured and our house isn't a target for high-end jewel thieves. Other than a couple of pieces I bought at a local art fair, there's little "real" gold, "real" silver, or "real" whatever that milky-purple stone is.

I splurged, though, on a beautiful jade-green necklace with a story behind it. The artist takes broken pieces of pottery and china and retools them.

If I ever become a jewelry designer—right after I fly solo over the North Pole or right after I swim the English Channel, which will be right after I dust my baseboards, become a better swimmer, and learn how to fly—I'm going to design a necklace I once wore in a dream.

Black as onyx but rough and unpolished, one stone is coal, followed by a light-catching, expertly cut round diamond. Then another lump of coal, another diamond, coal, diamond, coal, diamond. Coal on its own would leave dusty smudges on anyone wearing the necklace, so they're dipped in…something. Polyurethane?

Coal, diamond, coal, diamond.

The classic black-and-clear alternating pattern would go with anything. It *does* go with anything. It's the pattern of consequences (rough coal) and grace (light reflected in all directions). A gem of grace for every dark consequence.

That's the life we're offered. The rough, sharp-edged, smudging chunks of coal that represent the consequences of our choices are threaded on the sterling chain of life with matching graces.

Lord, I have regrets from childhood.

"I know. I have a grace for that."

I'm still conscious of how that decision in college left me with gaps in my education.

"I have a grace for that."

I wasn't always patient with my kids.

"Grace for that."

Or my husband.

"And that."

Despite my good intentions, I made a couple of bad choices about time usage yesterday.

"Grace."

And I forgot sunscreen more than I remembered it.

"Another gem of grace."

And a consequence?

"Both."

Coal. Diamond. Coal. Diamond.

"Exactly."

There's a grace to match my every need.

"In a way."

A way?

"Do the math."

As I take another look at the imaginary but very much real necklace of consequences, I notice a distinct imbalance. The array of stones both begins and ends with grace. Grace will always outnumber consequences. His grace is more than sufficient. — Cynthia

TODAY'S PRAYER

Father God, what a difference it makes to know that my life
is hemmed by grace. Fingers of Your grace weave through
all the consequences of my mistakes. I'm grateful, Lord.
Help me live so the grace parts sparkle.

Here, Wear My Armor!

*Saul replied, "You are not able to go out against
this Philistine and fight him; you are only a young man,
and he has been a warrior from his youth."*

1 SAMUEL 17:33

It took a lot of talking for David to convince King Saul that he could slay the giant. Even then, nervous Saul placed his tunic around the boy and added a suit of armor and a bronze helmet. But when David tried to walk around, he kept falling over from the weight of it. He rejected it all and went after Goliath armed with just a sling and some stones.

How many times have we faced challenges that look as big as that giant? We stand there, with our sling and stones, wishing we had a king to stand behind us and some armor or a helmet to protect us.

I often equate David's story to my own battle against ovarian cancer—although, when that phone call came to identify it as the Goliath standing before me, my attitude was far more Saul than David. I yearned for dependable armor or a big old helmet! When I pulled back the band of my sling, I realized I had no stone to load into it.

Then God's grace sent Dr. Alison Calkins, who was beautiful, smart, and compassionate. She looked me straight in the eyes and answered every one of my six thousand questions. She let me cry without judgment, and when my weight was more than the radiation machine would allow, she even figured out how to build a support. Through her and her team, God fashioned the little stone I needed to take one brazen shot at cancer.

I'll never forget the day Dr. Calkins told me, many weeks later, that the giant wasn't getting back up again. "You and I are going to be together for the rest of your life," she said with a smile, as she explained

how she envisioned my post-cancer care. "And I'm happy to tell you…
that will be a *very long time*."

Even now, more than six years later, I still feel queasy when I wait
at the light at Martin Luther King Boulevard to turn into St. Joseph's
Hospital for my annual checkup. At first, I remember the loneliness of
those treatments, the fear and the anxiety and the desperation. But as
I park in a spot marked RADIATION THERAPY PATIENTS ONLY and the
glass door slides open and I spot Connie or Alex or Ann Marie, my
heart starts to beat again. Excitedly, I anticipate seeing Dr. Calkins,
knowing she'll be the reminder God brings that the giant has been slain.

I'll bet, every now and then, David spotted a small stone at the
side of the road and couldn't help but smile, remembering what he and
God had done. If only I could tuck Dr. Calkins into my pocket and
carry her with me as a reminder: *By the grace of God, giants are slain!*
— Sandie

TODAY'S PRAYER

. . . .

Father God, I'm humbled by Your grace as I face
the towering giants in my life. You are always prepared
for them, and You invariably provide just what I need
for the fight, whether that be a stone
or a doctor with a sweet, promising smile.

"Good Enough" Never Is

But since you excel in everything—in faith, in speech, in knowledge,
in complete earnestness and in the love we have kindled in you—
see that you also excel in this grace of giving.

2 CORINTHIANS 8:7

Like most kids, I once had a love/hate relationship with Saturdays, because that's when Dad doled out allowances and Mom distributed the weekly chores list. And, like most kids, it didn't take long before I adopted a "whatever" attitude.

If a halfhearted flap didn't shake every lint ball from the scatter rugs, oh well, no one would care, right? Those lumps and bumps under my blankets? Hardly visible under a couple dozen carefully positioned stuffed animals!

When Mom pointed out that I hadn't dusted *under* the knick-knacks, I wondered who (besides her) would notice. And every time Dad frowned at the quickly folded handkerchiefs I'd stacked on top of his dresser, I wanted to say, "You're only gonna blow your nose on 'em, anyway..."

So it was that "Good Enough" became my mantra (even before I knew what a mantra *was),* and when I held out a sticky hand to collect my allowance, I didn't even have the good grace to feel guilty. And *that,* of course, inspired "Do Your Best" speeches from my parents, like:

Haste Makes Waste. ("You don't need that much furniture polish!")
Finish What You Start. ("You forgot to drain the dishwater. Again.")
Take Pride in Your Work. ("Is this your best work?")

To further compound things, our pastor tucked those very same adages into his sermons on Sunday mornings. One service in particular felt as though it had been written specifically for me and, thinking that my parents had put him up to it, I went into full preteen pout mode and stayed that way, even as I washed the dinner dishes. As it happened, it was my sister's turn to dry, and when a still-greasy glass I'd haphazardly "washed" slipped from her hand, she cut her finger while trying to pick up the pieces. A dozen parental lectures echoed in my head, and I grudgingly admitted that if I'd done my job properly, Claudia wouldn't have dropped the glass in the first place.

Finally, I "got" the message. By repeating my parents' lessons, the pastor had provided proof that the Lord *wanted* me to learn these things and intended to use every voice at His disposal to make sure I heard Him.

My mantra changed that day, from "Good Enough!" to "Good Enough Never Is."

As I guided my daughters through mundane chores and home-work, I shared lessons from my own childhood, and, as my parents and pastor had, I added Scripture to back up every word. "Everything you do and say," I told them, "echoes God's grace in you…

"so I pray—and you should too—that you'll always make a beautiful sound!" ⌐ Loree

TODAY'S PRAYER

. . . .

My heart overflows with gratitude, Lord, that You—
Creator of the universe—consider this lowly servant worthy
of Your loving lessons. Keep teaching me, Father, that I must
steep myself in Your Word. Bless me with an ever-faithful heart
and an obedient spirit, so that every move I make
and each word I utter echoes the grace and glory
of Your mighty and merciful love.

Little Ol' Me

*The LORD did not set his affection on you and choose you
because you were more numerous than other peoples,
for you were the fewest of all peoples.*

DEUTERONOMY 7:7

Fame is a funny thing. Despite the obvious annoyance of paparazzi, a publicist's dream is an increase in media exposure for her clients. One of the points of achieving fame is to appeal to the crowd mentality: if everyone's rushing to experience this [person, band, actor, film], there must be something special there! Of course we can all come up with at least one example of that crowd mentality showing itself wrong. Milli Vanilli comes to mind. Sir Mix-a-Lot. *Jersey Shore. The Real Housewives of* Anywhere.

But we do tend to put value in numbers that way.

So today's verse points out yet another way God sees things differently than the world. "Powerful" people or big numbers have never impressed Him. After all, when He first set apart the Israelites as His chosen people, Abraham, Sarah, and Isaac were the only members of that particular in-crowd. And although the Israelites slowly grew in number, many other ethnic groups were far larger and more powerful.

Historically, the point of today's verse was to bolster the spirits of the Israelites before they faced a mass of larger foes—the Hittites, Amorites, and a lot of other "ites." In essence, God told them, "Don't worry about the size of your enemy. I'm going to be there for you—not because you're big and powerful but because you're mine. I chose you because I love you—that's why I redeemed you from slavery."

I see much to embrace about this verse today as well. God extended that "chosen" status to "a thousand generations of those who love him and keep his commandments" (Deuteronomy 7:9). A thousand generations. Now there's a big number worth considering, because it eventually included us. Jesus came to earth with our redemption from slavery in His heart. Not because we're big shots or numerous, but because He loves us. Every single one of us, on an individual basis.

I tend to go through life with a rather healthy confidence and optimism, but on my worst days I might feel very small. I might doubt my real value to anyone. Maybe no one remembered my birthday or my favorite book idea got rejected. Perhaps someone gave a particularly negative book review or some smart-mouthed kid called me an old lady. Plenty of people might question their value for more serious reasons, like an unfaithful spouse, an abusive parent, or negligent and estranged kids. Maybe they're facing chronic illness or financial hardship.

It's easy enough to recognize God's love when everything is going our way. When appreciative friends and family surround us. When we're successful, maybe even achieving a modicum of fame. When our health is good and our accounts are in order. But God didn't set His affection on us and choose us for any of those reasons.

He *did* choose us, though, and He *does* love us—regardless of what the crowd might say. ⌒ Trish

TODAY'S PRAYER

Abba Father, I would be nothing without Your unfailing love. Thank You for choosing me. Please help me to remember Your love and to lean on Your grace, especially when I feel small and unimportant in the world. I love You.

With You, There Is Forgiveness

If you, LORD, kept a record of sins, Lord, who could stand?
But with you there is forgiveness, so that we can,
with reverence, serve you.

PSALM 130:3-4

The night was full of laughter, marked as one of the best adult fellowships on record for our church: Tacky Night.

Imagine a fellowship hall filled with fifty so-called adults dressed in the tackiest outfits they could find. I told my husband he could just pull one of his everyday flannel shirts from the closet and be okay. But he managed to "tacky" it up—or down—even more. I don't know what it says about us, but we adults rose to the challenge with a passion usually reserved for teen fads. No offense intended, teen fashionistas, but paying *extra* for holes in your jeans?

On Tacky Night, we wore things backward, inside out, upside down, layered to the point of insanity, garish, smudged, ripped, mismatched (good to know that's back in fashion), outdated, and old things that missed as fashion statements the first time around.

My husband and I looked at each other in the full-length mirror as we prepared to head to the event. Hmm. Not tacky enough. It was, after all, a competition for Tackiest Costume.

Ah! I had the answer. I hiked my seventies' granny skirt above my ankles and ran upstairs. I yanked open my dresser drawer, and there they were—the perfect accessories for my ensemble. My band medals.

What's tackier than a grown woman wearing a vest with her junior high and high school music competition medals pinned all over it?

"Thanks for asking. This one is a blue ribbon/gold medal for taking first place for my bassoon solo in eighth grade. And this one? Yes, that's for our woodwind quintet. First place at the state competition. And these three are for vocal awards—our double sextet, show choir, and duet. These six are from—"

Yeah. That's tacky all right.

I don't remember who won the competition for Tackiest Costume. The challenge brought out a talent for tacky most of us didn't realize we had.

Fun night. Lots of laughs.

But what if…?

What if the Lord made us publicly wear our offenses against Him, in a *Scarlet Letter* sort of way—all of them? What if I had to pin a hunk of metal on my vest for every potato chip I sneaked? What if I had to add more for every time I voiced my impatience? What if each misuse of time was marked in a visible way? What if all my mistakes as a child, as a mate, as a parent, as an employee formed individual "medals" I was forced to wear—all of them at once, every day, with every outfit? I'd be doubled over with the weight—the ultimate "fallen and I can't get up!" Lord, if You marked our transgressions, who could stand? ⌒ Cynthia

TODAY'S PRAYER

Lord God of immeasurable grace, thank You for keeping my failures to Yourself and then throwing them away. Thank You for taking divine delight in removing the weight of my sins rather than making me wear them as a constant reminder of who I'd be without Your grace and mercy.

The Truth Hurts...
at First

Whoever rebukes a person will in the end gain favor
rather than one who has a flattering tongue.
PROVERBS 28:23

My friend Jemelle doesn't mess around. If you're a person prone to fishing for compliments, Jemelle is the wrong side of that fishhook. If you ask her about the outfit you have on, you'd better be sure you really want to know! That new haircut feeling questionable to you? Don't ask her about it unless you're braced and ready for the reply.

I made what initially felt like a very big mistake one night when I whined to her over dinner about my struggles with weight loss. "It seems like I just can't make any progress," I told her. "One step forward and two steps back."

I suddenly had the feeling she'd been holding back her feelings on the subject for a long time and I'd just handed over the key to the lecture room.

"That's because you're only half committed," she began. "You need to really look at what you're eating. Your food choices just aren't healthy. You're never going to reach your goal doing it this way." A half hour later, her lecture left me feeling a little like a waterlogged bystander caught up in a flood.

But that night after she left my house, I couldn't sleep. I blamed the caffeine in the diet Cokes I'd consumed. Then I blamed Jemelle. Who did she think she was? What did this gorgeous woman know about a weight problem like mine?

The next day, her words danced around in my head like one of those songs you just can't shake. I grabbed some chocolate, curled up in a chair, and really worked on being mad at her all afternoon. It went on like that for nearly a week…until the voice of God in my spirit told me what I already knew.

I called Jemelle and opened with, "If I ask you a question, will you promise not to hold it against me later?" It was no surprise when she replied, "No."

"I need your help," I told her—four little words that set into motion an avalanche of support, encouragement, tips, and advice that I rely upon heavily to this day, years later.

Next to other friends—*wonderful friends!*—willing to help me make my excuses, who play down my concerns with polite courtesy or uncomfortable silences, she can seem pretty harsh at times. But the truth is this: Jemelle has no interest in flattering me or making me feel comfortable in my own skin. Her concern is having me around; she wants me to be present at her children's birthday parties and at family gatherings (which always include me). She wants us to enjoy our lives together.

No, it isn't always easy to hear what Jemelle has to say. But I've come to believe that every person—male or female, fat or thin, old or young—absolutely *must* have a Jemelle in their life to tell them the truth when no one else can or will. I wouldn't trade this woman for all the chocolate in the Ghirardelli factory. And that's sayin' somethin'!

— Sandie

TODAY'S PRAYER

Thank You, Jesus, for grace that comes by way
of the truth-tellers in life. Let me always hear them
with spiritual ears and a godly heart.

A Little Brass-O
Goes a Long Way

*Listen, my dear brothers and sisters: Has not God chosen those who
are poor in the eyes of the world to be rich in faith and to inherit
the kingdom he promised those who love him?*

JAMES 2:5

My dad served as an usher at church, helping folks find seats, passing collection plates, making sure the hymnals and pencils were tucked away, and walking elderly parishioners to their cars once services ended. He was so dedicated that the pastor presented him with a brass badge. In bold, black letters above his name, it said HEAD USHER.

Blushing, Dad endured the hand-shaking congratulations of the other ushers and thanked them all—the good reverend in particular—and tucked the badge into his pocket. As he was a former soldier, they believed him when he said there wasn't time to put it on "good and straight."

Well, Dad never put it on, good and straight or any other way. When the preacher and his fellow ushers asked why, he'd chuckle and say, "Forgot to buff off the Brass-o!" and "Must have left it in my loose-change tray."

After dinner one Sunday, I asked Dad why he refused to wear the bright and shiny name tag.

"Well," he began, "you know how I've always said that when we donate old clothes, we must never let anyone see us deliver the bags to the church?"

I nodded. "Because it might embarrass the poor people."

"That, and because a good deed never makes you feel as good as when it's done in private."

41

"You mean, like when Mrs. Smitherman taught us that God wants us to pray in the closet so people won't think we're being all show-offy with our fine and fancy words?"

Laughing, he said, "Exactly! The reward isn't in the admiration of others, but in knowing you've done the right thing for the right reason."

That made sense. But what did it have to do with his refusal to wear the badge?

"Service to the church is like praying…or putting my weekly tithe into an envelope before dropping it into the collection plate. I don't help out so that the pastor and others will think better of me. I do it so *I'll* think better of me."

I still didn't get it and said so.

"God knows when our hearts are right, and mine feels right when I'm in service to Him."

"So…the reward isn't in the admiration of others," I echoed, tacking on my own ending. "It's in heaven."

"Exactly," he repeated. Then he reached into his pocket, withdrew the name tag, and pressed it into my palm. He didn't say a word, but I got the message loud and clear.

I'll treasure that badge all the days of my life, not because it's made of polished brass, but because it's a shiny reminder that with a "right heart," we can please the Father, who has graced us with so many blessings, great and small! — Loree

TODAY'S PRAYER
. . . .

Bless me, Father, with a humble heart and a grace-filled spirit,
that I might always give generously and quietly as You would
have me do, for the only praise and admiration I need
to seek will come from You when I arrive in paradise.

Warmer by the Fire

"So you will be my people, and I will be your God."
JEREMIAH 30:22

Lately, I've been a little overwhelmed—not so much by what's going on in my own life, but by the struggles of many of my friends and acquaintances. That's one of the by-products of our easy access to communication with people all over the world. Any one of us only needs to be on a prayer loop or Facebook, let alone watch the news, to understand how hard life is for many people.

It's gotten to the point that, each time I come across another prayer request, I have to simply stop what I'm doing and offer up a prayer right there and then. Otherwise, I know those requests and needs will get lost on my ever-growing list.

And I've had my own share of turmoil to deal with. Who hasn't, right?

"So you will be my people, and I will be your God." God made this promise quite a number of times to the Israelites in the Old Testament. And thanks to Christ's sacrifice for us, believing Gentiles have been given the same promise.

So how do we rectify the two situations? Why do so many of us suffer hardships in life if we've been given the blessing of being God's people? When I truly stop to consider the promise in that verse, it doesn't say a doggone thing about my life being easier or free of unemployment, illness, or heartache. It merely says I'm one of God's people.

Merely.

Just imagine facing whatever you face or have faced without the unbelievable honor of being His. When I think of how events might have unfolded in my own life—especially the tougher parts of it—without His looking after me? It makes me shiver.

That makes me think about dark and bitter winter nights—I'm most definitely *not* a winter person—and that feeling of sitting with my back to the fireplace to fight the cold. I mean, I'm spoiled by the comfort of my home and the availability of heat—I know that. But still. When I'm cold, I feel tension down to my bones and all up through my shoulders and neck—just full-body tension. But sitting near that fire… ah, coziness, peace, comfort… And then there's that reluctant moment when I have to get up and walk away from the fire and I feel the cold envelop me again. It's always warmer by the fire.

No matter what I might face today or in the future, I hope I will always remember the words right before today's verse. " 'For who is he who will devote himself to be close to me?' declares the LORD" (Jeremiah 30:21). Surely any loss, pain, battle, or fear that comes along will be easier to endure, the closer I am to Him.

As much as I can, I want to devote myself to getting as close to Him as possible. And that's what I'll pray for others. ⟶ Trish

TODAY'S PRAYER

Gracious God, thank You so much that You have made me
Yours. You already know whatever challenges I'll have
in my future. Please help me remember to devote myself
to being as close to You as I can, and I pray that for others too.

Hazards

Though I walk in the midst of trouble, you preserve my life.
PSALM 138:7

With the agility of a woman half my age—*okay, a third. Let's give that woman a true advantage*—I nimbly stepped over the trip wire, then pivoted to avoid the camouflaged danger designed to maim. I pulled out my Lamaze breathing to slow my heart rate. *Stay calm. Stay…calm.*

Balancing on one foot, I leaned forward, my arms a tightrope-walker's pole. I made an adjustment. Steady… Whew. Safely over another obstacle. But there was no relaxing yet. Metal and ball bearings—a dangerous combination—lay between me and an oasis of relative safety.

What was that? Quicksand? Great. *Resist the urge to struggle. Slow movements.* Muscles taut, I grabbed the arm of the couch with one hand and the end table with the other. Yes! Free from the gauntlet of dangers, I scraped Play-Doh off the bottom of my Nikes and headed for the kitchen to make lunch for the grandkids.

I'd successfully dodged Matchbox cars, marbles, Legos, and Mr. Potato Head parts.

But the kitchen wasn't the safe haven for which I'd hoped. And hopped.

One grandson knelt on all fours on the floor, eating Cheerios from a bowl he pretended was a dog dish.

Another grandson had found the ice cream pail of birdseed. The gallon size. He's grown so clever, that boy. I didn't know he'd learned how to pop the lid off an ice cream pail—or that he was so skilled at pouring. In some cultures, the pattern of birdseed piles on the hardwood floor would count as art. But birdseed is slippery, piled up like that. One more obstacle to navigate. Distracted from the danger, I briefly wondered if the blue jays and goldfinches at the birdfeeder would mind if their dinner was first swept off the floor.

The sound of the river swelled to a roar. *Wait a minute. There's no river in the bathroom.* My mistake. There was now.

Some days, life's obstacles are no more threatening than hidden Legos and Play-Doh land mines. Other times, the ring of the telephone is the emotional equivalent of a tornado warning or tsunami alert. *The tests don't look good. We'll have to schedule a biopsy. This is the last resort. If rehab doesn't work for her this session, she'll face jail-time. Sorry, but we're laying off people with far more seniority than you. I'm sorry we couldn't do more for your mother. All we can do now is try to keep her comfortable.*

Those calls have come, with varying outcomes, too many times in the last few years.

Always, they were accompanied by miracles. We either skirted the danger or were carried through it. What a rush it is to feel the grip of grace around us as God dodges threats we can't even see. We may be dizzied by His maneuvers, but we're held. ⌐ Cynthia

TODAY'S PRAYER
. . . .

Lord God, I can't imagine what's hiding in the carpet of this day, this week, this year. All I know is that You know, and that's enough. Together, we've crossed some frightening territory, haven't we? You've proved Your faithfulness in every episode. I was healed or held or both. Thank You, Lord. Make me as agile as You are, light on my feet and light in my heart, while we run this gauntlet called life.

Peace of Mind: Not Just for Greeting Cards

Then he returned to his disciples and found them sleeping.
"Couldn't you men keep watch with me for one hour?"
MATTHEW 26:40

Recently, I went through a rough time. I received a lot of online and snail-mail greeting cards from wonderful friends that spoke to finding "peace of mind" and "resting in God's arms." But peace hadn't been easily found in recent months. God felt distant and far-off.

"Please," I beseeched Him often. "I need some grace. Mercy."

One afternoon, with the television blaring and my third cup of coffee brewing in the Keurig, it suddenly occurred to me that I was starved for some silence. From the time the alarm sounded in the morning until the moment I drifted off to sleep to the hum of the late-evening news, some form of noise had kept me company for weeks.

So I turned off the television, and I sat down in my favorite chair and closed my eyes.

"I miss You, Lord," I whispered. "Please. I need You."

The twelve-year-old next door dribbled his basketball and plunked it against their garage door. His mother set the alarm on her SUV for the umpteenth time. A motor revved. The coffee pot belched. Another neighbor's toddler began to wail.

"Shh," I told my environment. "Please."

The phone rang, and I ignored it. My cell phone jingled with a text. The dog tossed a squeaky toy at me.

"Lord, *please*. I can't think over all the noise."

I heard a sweet, slightly sarcastic reply, deep down in my spirit. "Gee, I wonder how *that* feels."

I set my Bible on my knee and began to read. It took me several minutes before I realized that it had been at least two weeks since I'd cracked it open. And aside from a few "please"-oriented sentences tossed upward, when had I last sat down at His feet and truly prayed?

I spent the next hour talking to Jesus. I laid out the events of recent weeks before Him as if He hadn't been there to experience it all. I cried so hard that my ears plugged up when I blew my nose afterward. I slid open the glass door to the backyard, and a warm Florida breeze kissed my face. I closed my eyes and enjoyed an undercurrent of blissful silence that was marred only by the lyrical music of a song that no one but me could audibly hear:

"I love you.... I am with you.... You are the apple of My eye.... You are not alone."

From that afternoon on, I have made it a point to devote some time each day to being quiet before God. Even if it's only for fifteen minutes in my car or in my bedroom or in the garage while waiting for the dryer to stop, I breathe, I am quiet, and I listen. Sometimes my thoughts are interrupted by the noise of the day, but always I draw nearer to God. And those few minutes belong just to us. They are the most exquisite few minutes of every single day. —Sandie

TODAY'S PRAYER

Lord Jesus, help us to be quiet enough to listen to the still, small voice that has so much to say, if we'll only be silent long enough to hear.

Forever Young

Even to your old age and gray hairs
I am he, I am he who will sustain you.
I have made you and I will carry you;
I will sustain you and I will rescue you.

ISAIAH 46:4

At the drugstore, while I was trying to decide between a musical birthday card and one of its less-noisy cousins, a lively lady stepped up beside me and said, "*You* look like a friendly gal…"

A pink-painted fingernail tapped a box of Light Golden Blond. "I've been wearing this shade since high school," she whispered, "but I *sooo* need a change!" Giving Lightest Ash Blond a shake, she arched an eyebrow. "Now, be honest, honey—which looks best?"

As if scripted by Spielberg, the song "Forever Young" wafted from the ceiling speakers. Ignoring the irony, I said, "With your pretty blue eyes and pale complexion, the lighter color will look very flattering."

She thanked me with a card-crushing hug. "Buy the Popeye card," she suggested. "My nephew loved it!"

I turned back to the greeting cards and caught a glimpse of myself in the mirror atop the sunglasses rack. My dark roots and smile lines sent me directly to the hair-color aisle…and then the skin care department. (An ounce of balm is worth a pound of wrinkles, right?) Last stop, the makeup aisle, for a tube of concealer that, according to TV commercials and magazine ads, would camouflage the telltale signs of my peculiar schedule.

On my way to the checkout, I stared at the products in my cart. *Lord*, I prayed silently, *what'll this cost, not only in dollars, but in time spent applying it? And what makes me think* any *of it will keep me forever young?*

His gentle answer came in the form of the elderly woman who shuffled across my path, reminding me of my years working for a nursing home, where white hair, thinning skin, and age spots were tributes to lives well lived. Every wrinkle, a line connecting them with a moment from the past; each silvery hair, proof of a lesson learned. And behind farsighted lenses, eyes that sparkled with wisdom as arthritis-gnarled fingers followed lines of Scripture in worn Bibles.

Once, over the lunchtime din in the dining room, I overheard a woman whimper about being confined to a wheelchair. "Try to be more like King David," said her tablemate. "He didn't focus on the size of the obstacles he faced, but on the saving grace of his Maker."

"Now that," the Almighty seemed to be telling me, *"is how to grow old gracefully."* I realized that the ravages of time can't mar the *outside* of me, because through the grace of the Father, I'm forever changed *on the inside.*

At home, while unpacking my purchases, the Popeye card opened and blasted me with a hearty "I Am What I Am."

And this time, I didn't ignore the irony. ⌁ Loree

TODAY'S PRAYER
. . . .

Thank You, Father, for carrying me—from the moment
I was born—in Your strong and loving arms.
Never let me forget that although the years may slow my pace
and line my face, they cannot erase Your Word,
which You've written on my heart.

Obviously!

*May these words of my mouth and this meditation of my heart
be pleasing in your sight, LORD, my Rock and my Redeemer.*

PSALM 19:14

Some things are just obvious. Like sunshine. I've seen sunshine often enough to know it's out there, even on a cloudy day. Believe me, I have the age spots to prove it.

And the stars are obvious too. I don't often consider the stars during the day, but they're in the sky, regardless of the fact that I can't see them.

The physical heavens are all part of God's majestic creation, and everyone in the world is witness to them. In Psalm 19, David says it doesn't matter where you plant your feet or what language you speak; you see these obvious wonders. They're easy to spot and identify.

He says something similar about God's laws. We may not always be sure about God's will for our future, but because God's laws are spelled out in the Bible, His will with regard to our behavior is obvious. "The law of the LORD is perfect," David says. "More precious than gold" and "sweeter than honey." Yep, this psalm includes those famous words too.

Granted, some Old Testament laws are confusing. In 2005, A. J. Jacobs, Senior Editor of *Esquire* magazine, attempted to follow as many of the Old Testament laws as he could for one year. Some he simply found hard to understand—the ban against mixing particular fibers when making cloth; the ban on shaving one's beard; the ban on certain moves by a wife fighting on behalf of her husband. Imagine— they had Jerry Springer moments back then!

Jacobs understood other laws but found them hard to consistently obey—as most of us do. No gossiping, cursing, lying, or working on Sunday (or whatever day one honors as the Sabbath).

Confusing laws aside, God's will about most of our moral dilemmas is clear, thanks to the Ten Commandments. I needn't look far to know that He wants to be my only god. He doesn't want me to murder or commit adultery. He wants me to honor Mom and Dad. Like the sun and the stars, His laws exist whether I acknowledge them or not.

So. God's creation? Obvious!

God's laws? Obvious!

My faults? Uhh. David says those can get a little fuzzy, and I have to agree. Sometimes I fool even myself about what's going on in my heart. In Psalm 19, David asks God to forgive his "hidden faults," and he didn't mean that those faults were hidden from *God.* I have the ability to ignore my own selfish motives, my jealous innermost thoughts, and my true angry feelings. Like David, I need to continually ask for God's grace and guidance—to say, "May these words of my mouth and this meditation of my heart be pleasing in your sight." ⌒ Trish

TODAY'S PRAYER

. . . .

Father God, Your majesty is so evident in the world You've
created. Your desire that our lives be free of strife is clear
by the laws you provide for us. And Your gracious patience
with us—with me, Lord, and my obvious and hidden faults—
is constant and hard to fathom. Please help me to see
honestly into my heart and to always
speak words that honor You.

Take a Deep Breath

Let us then approach God's throne of grace with confidence,
so that we may receive mercy and find grace
to help us in our time of need.

HEBREWS 4:16

I took a deep breath and blew out the flames. Flames. My car was on fire. And my toddler kids were inside.

How it happened, we're still not sure.

The trip home from Grandma's started simply enough. The first few miles were uneventful. The next few revealed the reason why I didn't consider my kids the world's best travelers. Singing an endless litany of songs to toddlers strapped into kid prison (car seats) against their will and too close to one another in the backseat, I dodged road hazards and sibling disagreements. If I'd had any, I'd have dug into my purse for blood-pressure pills. Instead, I dug for more mom-grace and patience.

From above, the highway must have looked like an asphalt amusement ride—steep inclines, tight curves, warnings to hang onto the safety bar, er, steering wheel…

The miles crawled by. As moms do, I focused what I hoped was equal attention on maneuvering the deteriorating relationship in the backseat with the narrow shoulders and sprinkling of dead animals beyond the windshield. Skunks. Raccoons. Deer.

An unmistakable odor seeped into the car's interior. Yes, I'd have to change the youngest's diaper at our next stop. But there was some otherworldly smell that had nothing to do with roadkill.

Burning rubber. Like flip-flops too close to a bonfire.

Fire?

No, kids, I will not sing another round of "The Wheels on the Bus."
One of ours is on fire at the moment. Give Mommy a minute.

I pulled the car onto a wide stretch of cement—the lot of a gas
station. Now that I think about it, flames and thousands of gallons
of gasoline don't make great neighbors. Next time, I'll choose a less-
flammable location when my car's on fire.

My heart racing, I bounded out of the car and traced the smoke
and flames to the left front wheel. A tire should not crackle and snap
like a birch log in a fireplace. But maybe that's just my opinion.

The sight of the flames—appreciably more pronounced than the
birthday-candle variety—and the nearness of my children made me
forget I couldn't do it. So I did. I took a quick, deep breath accompanied by a quick, deep prayer and blew out the flames.

I don't think that's even possible…but I did it.

The safety of my kids was at stake. I found superhuman-lung-
capacity-grace to help in a time of need. I approached the front of the
car boldly, even if less than confidently, and found grace to help in a
time of—

I don't think that's exactly what the writer of the book of Hebrews
meant when he penned the words we lean on. But I understand the
concept better since the fire. ⟶ Cynthia

TODAY'S PRAYER

Lord of all, God of wonders far beyond our galaxy, thank You
for all the times You intervene in my ordinary days with
extraordinary displays of Your grace. Thank You for
empowering me both when the stakes are high and when
the flames are high. Thanks for the reminder that Your grace
is always there and always greater than my need.

Give Me a Sign!

"He rescues and he saves;
he performs signs and wonders
in the heavens and on the earth."

DANIEL 6:27

Did you ever notice how the Lord sets up road signs along the highways of our lives? I think this was one of my earliest revelations about my faith walk: Pay attention, and God will lead.

I'm one of those people who gets lost pretty much everywhere I go. I'm sort of known for it. For this reason, one of my closest friends has taken on the role of GPS in my life. If I'm headed somewhere new, he'll often send me an e-mail with written directions that read something like this: "Take a left at Robertson Avenue. The street sign there is obscured, so it sneaks up on you, but you'll know it by the Shell station on the corner." David knows that the little details can make or break me.

Jesus knows this about me too.

Early on in my writing career, I only knew that I wanted to write. I had a very clear vision of the day my Creator crafted me for future life, whispering into my ear what He would have me do: *"Writer."* But that's where the clarity ended. I took a disorganized cluster-bomb approach, tossing everything I had at the wall to see if anything might stick. I tried writing sexy romance novels, scary suspense, screenplays, short stories, magazine articles, even advertising copy. If an opportunity arose to put words on a page, I engaged.

How many times have you asked, "Why did You put this desire and ability in me only to have it waste away without success?" After a gazillion instances where I asked that very question, it occurred to me that He is not a God who wastes words. If He'd really breathed *"Writer"* into me, He may have actually had a plan for me to accomplish it.

With that revelation, I began to watch the signs more closely. If an opportunity arose, I prayed, weighed, considered, asking, "What is my final destination?" *To serve God through my writing.* "How do I get there?" *By watching for the signs that lead me down that specific road.* For many writers, magazine articles and jingles make sense as part of their journey. For me and my path, however, that isn't the case. It was a long, messy road to this focus, but two years after I reached it, I sold my first romantic comedy to the inspirational market. WELCOME TO YOUR DESTINY. *At last.*

Situations often arise that require me to unfold the map again, measuring opportunity against final outcome: "Does this contribute to my journey?" If so, great! If not, I have to find a way to do what we women often have a hard time doing—I must say "No, thank you; that's not for me" and be on my way. With this kind of focus about where I'm headed, I'm able to make solid decisions that won't waste precious time and energy or break my stride. ⌁ Sandie

TODAY'S PRAYER

Help me today, sweet Jesus, to take the time to listen
and watch for Your guidance. Don't let me drift too far
from Your plan for me, and help me not to contribute
to someone else's wrong turns.

It Isn't a Stick!

That person is like a tree planted by streams of water,
which yields its fruit in season and whose leaf does not wither—
whatever they do prospers.

PSALM 1:3

Isn't it amazing how easily the maple trees' "whirlybirds" take root? Not long ago, I transplanted one that had grown into a magnificent red-leafed sapling. When the digging was done, I sat back to admire the Lord's handiwork while sipping lemonade and reading the mail, which included a home-improvement catalog. There on page ten was a full-color, 5 x 7 photo of a shiny green-and-yellow, ultra-quiet, mulching lawn mower. With a padded handle. And chrome spokes. *Be still my heart!*

That evening when my hubby asked, "What do you want for your birthday this year?" I pointed to the mower of my dreams, which came as no surprise to the man who has fulfilled past birthday, Christmas, and anniversary requests with compound miter saws, hammer drills, ratchet sets, and plumb bobs. "Let's take a little drive after supper," he said, "and we'll get your fancy mower." *Thank you, Lord, for blessing me with a husband who understands me!* The next morning I rolled my new mower from the shed.

Now seems as good a time as any to admit that I'm a bit impatient—and a symptom of my impatience is an aversion to reading directions. *It's a lawn mower,* I thought, pulling the START cord. How different could it be from others I'd owned and loved?

Suffice it to say, the manufacturers weren't kidding when they stamped SELF-PROPELLED on the handle. The minute I fired it up, that baby took off like a rocket, and in the blink of an eye, my newly relocated red-leafed maple went from five feet to a mere six inches in height.

I said my apologies—to the tree and its Creator—for the demolition my "who needs directions?" mind-set had caused, and pledged to bring it back. Every moment thereafter spent watering, fertilizing, pruning, and staking reminded me of the destructive aftereffects of my impatience. As I prayed for God to save the little tree, I also prayed He'd rid me of the arrogance that feeds my impatience.

His grace is stunning, indeed, for just as He saved my sinful soul with the promise of salvation I had not earned, He healed that little tree. Within days, it grew an inch, and emerald sprouts peeked from the mower-scratched bark! One evening my husband noticed the still-spindly stalk. "Whatever possessed you to plant a stick in the middle of the yard?" he asked.

"It *isn't* a stick," I said. "It's my newest tool, and I'm using it to measure my personal growth."

As he walked away scratching his head, I smiled and sent a silent *Thank You* heavenward. Because I knew that tomorrow, when I fired up my nifty new lawn edger, I intended to read the directions! ~ Loree

TODAY'S PRAYER

Thank You, Lord, for the gift of Your healing grace.
Day by day, it is transforming me from a bare-branched sapling
into a full-flowering tree, with roots that search deep
into Your Word for the water and nourishment
that sustains my soul. Keep me hungry and reaching for You,
Father, all the days of my life.

Jordan, Jericho, and Just My Own Stuff

"Have I not commanded you? Be strong and courageous.
Do not be afraid; do not be discouraged,
for the LORD your God will be with you wherever you go."

JOSHUA 1:9

In a few months, my financial situation is going to undergo a significant change. That doesn't make me different from many other people, especially in these days of crazy financial fluctuation in our country. At least I have forewarning, which is proving to be both a blessing and a curse. On one hand, I know exactly when I need to take on the new financial burden, so I'm taking as many steps as I can to secure my nest egg and increase my income. On the other hand, I often wake in the middle of the night stressing over how I'll handle it. *Whether* I'll handle it.

What I'm experiencing is probably a teeny-tiny version of what Joshua felt when he knew he had to take over for Moses and get the Israelites across the Jordan and into the Promised Land. At least I don't have throngs of people leaning on me. Nor do I have an icon like Moses to live up to.

In this first chapter, God commands Joshua four times to "be strong and courageous." Well, okay, I can do that. Until a little later, when I again think about the future and break out in a sweat over how slowly I'm preparing, despite my best efforts. Then I need to toughen up once more, remember Joshua's challenge, and exhort myself to be strong and courageous.

But what if that's just not my nature? I mean, I have courage in certain things, and I'm thankful for it. Birthin' babies certainly wasn't for sissies. Neither was raising them to be healthy in mind, body, and spirit. Surviving a pretty scary marital relationship required fortitude and courage on many occasions.

Still, I think of the challenges that friends, acquaintances, and entire nations of people face—cancer, loss of loved ones, war, famine— and realize their call to courage is far more daunting than mine. How do they *do* it?

How did Joshua do it? Once he led the Israelites across the Jordan, he had to overthrow kingdoms already established in the Promised Land. And he succeeded at all of his God-commanded tasks by taking one step at a time and trusting God's guidance with unshakable obedience, right down to marching around an enemy fortress seven times and tooting horns in order to make it fall down.

We all have our Jordans to cross. We all face fortresses of varying sizes at points in our lives. While my trials may pale in comparison to someone else's, they're still my trials. Or maybe I face a task more overwhelming than someone else's. God knows all about it. If I can remember to keep putting Him at the center of each day, each effort— to pray, search His Word, and seek His will—I'll cross that river. I'll win whatever battle I see on my own personal horizon. He'll be with me, wherever I go. ⌐ Trish

TODAY'S PRAYER

· · · · · · · · · · · · · · · · · · · ·

Heavenly Father, You know the future I face and how much strength and courage I need to get by. Help me to always seek that strength and courage from You.

Scenic Overlook

*Fools show their annoyance at once
but the prudent overlook an insult.*

PROVERBS 12:16

If sixty is the new fifty and charcoal is the new black, is rude the new polite?

I watch HGTV when I'm in the kitchen. It helps to keep my mind off what sometimes takes on an air of drudgery—making a meal. I love to cook, especially the day after grocery shopping when the pantry and fridge are full of interesting possibilities. But I must admit, the responsibility doesn't always produce joy. Sometimes it screams, "Do I have to?"

I've seen several episodes of *House Hunters, House Hunters International, My First Place,* and other shows where prospective buyers view houses and condos before purchase. Watching is a geography lesson, an architectural lesson, a cultural lesson, and a lesson in "Whatever happened to common courtesy?"

The young couple from the East Coast looking to buy their first bungalow declares that their first place *must* have four bedrooms, three baths, a pool, a walk-in closet, granite countertops, and outdoor space. When they walk through the first showing, the young woman says, "I hate that color. Oh, this wallpaper is hideous!" The young man says, "They call this a garage?"

Contrast that with the British couple looking to purchase a vacation home in the south of France. Never losing their contented expressions, the couple picks their way through the rubble of a fixer-upper to the tenth power, making comments like, "This is a bit of a tight spot, isn't it?" "I should think a coat of paint would freshen this room a mite." "No indoor facilities? Well, that will take a moment of getting used to."

Yes, the British seem to have a natural grace about their approach to life, but the contrast makes me wonder how it became okay with many Americans to drop politeness in favor of brash annoyance.

We act as if a line of more than two in front of us is a personal insult. We fling names at those who irritate us by committing offenses as "large" as jamming the photocopier or taking the last cookie.

And our unspoken goal seems to be speed of annoyance. The faster we react, the more scathing our response, the stronger we are? Not according to God's Word. It's a fool who shows his annoyance at once. The smart ones, the strong of character, by God's standards, are those who choose to overlook an insult.

That probably means I should overlook the fact that my husband ate three bites of the pork chops I made last week and said, "Did you... did you do something different with the seasoning on these?"

"No. I used the same spice blend I used on the pork roast you liked so much last Sunday. Why?"

He scrunched his nose. "These taste weird."

When I said the meat seemed okay to me, he offered that maybe my taste buds were out of whack because of my head cold.

I think I'll overlook that. ↜ Cynthia

TODAY'S PRAYER
. . . .

Lord God who exercises perfect patience, thank You for
being patient with me while I learn to do life Your way.
And thank You for a husband who knew how important it was
to tell me he liked the chicken last night.

It's All Relative

"Because he loves me," says the LORD, "I will rescue him;
I will protect him, for he acknowledges my name."

PSALM 91:14

Perspective has a lot to do with how we handle the victories and failures we encounter along the way. And I believe that perspective's greatest influence comes by grace—the kind of grace that changes our landscape.

Have you ever faced a mountain so big that you found yourself just sitting there and staring at it rather than figuring out a way to cross it? Perhaps you arrived at the base of that mountain by way of a bad medical report, the loss of a loved one, or an unfathomable betrayal. Whatever the source of your obstacle, at first blush, your initial reaction probably involved surrender. Most of us are programmed that way. Even if we don't stay in surrender mode, the inclination is most definitely there. But then something happens, doesn't it?

I like to think of that "something" as grace provided by a God who knew all about the mountain before we ever turned the corner to face it. In the middle of the night, an answer comes. Or after days of tears and anxiety, a new day dawns and there is a change of heart, a shift of perspective. It's supernatural, isn't it?

I love the story of young David. While everyone else was devastated at the thought of a giant, talking to one another about certain defeat and the possibility of surrender, David had a revelation that came by the very grace of God.

"I think I know the answer!" he may have exclaimed. "I know how to scale the mountain before us!"

Oh, how they must have laughed at him. This audacious little squirt with a sling and a stone was going to slay the giant? Was he joking, or simply insane? Talk about delusions of grandeur!

While everyone else had decided the giant was just too big to defeat, the Lord supplied David with a very different perspective. Yes, the giant was big. But the good news: he was too big to *miss*. And so that little upstart with the big vision picked up a stone, loaded his sling, and with one shot he took the mighty giant down. Can you imagine the noise of the impact when that giant hit the ground, beneath the thunder of celebration from all the naysayers?

The next time you're faced with an unanticipated mountain—or a really, really big giant—try to look at it from a different angle. What can you learn from this? What purpose does this giant serve in your life? The limitless grace of God is going to carry you through the battle. And the best part of it all is that every battle serves a purpose. Maybe, like David, you'll emerge on the other side to find that it has played some integral part in the overall plan God has for your life. ∽ Sandie

TODAY'S PRAYER
· · · · · · · · · · · · · · · · · · · ·

Lord, help me today to see the tormenting giants through
Your eyes. Remind me that You have given me everything
I need to enter into battle, if necessary...and that the shelter
of Your wings will hide me if it's not that time.
Your protection and grace know no bounds.
What an awesome reality!

Shalom to Your Nefesh!

The LORD replied, "My Presence will go with you,
and I will give you rest."

EXODUS 33:14

I pulled another all-nighter again last night and spent a few of those hours playing my favorite Bible game. It's where I close my eyes, open to any page, let my forefinger draw circles in the air, then come to rest on a random passage. I'm always astounded at how God uses this as a means to answer prayer or guide decisions. (Or keep me awake when I have deadlines to meet!)

So, last night, when verse after verse about the Sabbath presented themselves, I was confused, because it wasn't Sunday. Was the Lord trying to tell me to pray for my dear Jewish friend, who celebrates every *Shabbat* as if it's Christmas or Easter?

Like her ancestors (and you and me), Shalva accepts as truth that we each have a *nefesh,* or soul. She also sees the world as a giant ticking clock that threatens to steal the calm and serenity required to draw close and commune with Him—not surprising for a woman whose very name means *tranquillity.* Shalva is adamant in her belief that all God's children need to obey His command to spend the Shabbat seeking the peace and quiet required to rest our tired spirits and renew our bodies.

After a phone call assured me that all was well in Shalva's world, I explained the real reason for my call. "So," she said, laughing, "He used me well, then." I didn't get it and said so. "Please," came her good-natured retort, "with the schedule you keep? I'm sure He's trying to make you understand that we *all* need to sleep. Why, even God Himself rested on the Sabbath!"

"But it isn't Sunday," I repeated.

Instead of the Old Testament references I expected to hear, she told me about a book she had read, written by her friend who'd recently returned from a church-sponsored trip to Africa. The missionaries hired natives to help carry supplies and made excellent time on the first leg of their journey. On the second morning, however, the men refused to move—a major disappointment to the eager-to-spread-the-word Christians. When asked why they insisted upon sitting and resting, their leader explained that because they'd moved too fast the day before, they needed to wait for their souls to catch up with their bodies.

"It's about balance," Shalva said in her quiet way. "It's important to allow ourselves to recover from life's too-fast pace…and it doesn't *always* have to happen on a Sunday."

Yes, even God Himself rested on the Sabbath. Not because creating the world had exhausted Him, but because, like a loving Father, He hoped to teach us by example the importance of nurturing ourselves—body, mind, and soul.

Tonight, when I lay down my head and close my eyes, I know I'll smile as I wish myself "Shalom!" I'll be praying that the grace of God will envelope *you* with peace too! ⸺ Loree

TODAY'S PRAYER
. . . .

Dear heavenly Father, I thank You for making sure—
even though I don't deserve it—that I can always learn Your
intentions for my life, whether through the words of the Bible
or the gentle voice of friends like Shalva.

Put Down That Remote

*"I, even I, am he who blots out your transgressions for my own sake,
and remembers your sins no more."*

ISAIAH 43:25

Hello, my name is Trish, and I'm a DVR addict.

Honestly, I don't know how I managed my ever-important television viewing before I had the amazing abilities of the Digital Video Recorder at my fingertips.

If a hot news story comes on while I'm taking a phone call, I can relax, knowing I can rewind to catch the news after I finish talking.

If I can't tell what a character just said because he's too cool to enunciate, I can not only rewind, but I can turn on captioning, letting my machine figure everything out for me and spoon-feed me my entertainment.

If I want to see how a particular special effect is accomplished, I can rewind and play it back frame by frame, until I thoroughly analyze the technique used to fool me into believing what the director would have me believe.

Best of all, if someone walks between me and the television right in the middle of something riveting, it doesn't matter. I remain calm, pick up my remote, rewind, and watch it again.

I wasn't always so attached to my DVR. The addiction crept up on me slowly. I learned how dependent I had become when I went to the theater with my son. It was a sci-fi film, and my mind wandered during an explanation that was important to the plot. So I started to ask my son to rewind for me before I caught myself. I realized that whatever I hadn't heard was lost forever. Or at least until I could rent the movie and watch it at home while clutching my DVR remote.

Aren't you relieved that God doesn't view our lives and behavior that way? I mean, clearly He has total control over the time-space continuum, so if He were inclined, He could glance back at any point in my life and review my bad choices, my appalling behavior, my sins. He could gel in His mind the times I completely disregarded or dishonored Him. He could easily compile a list of reasons why I shouldn't be of any concern to Him, not here on earth or forever in heaven.

But He chooses not to do that. He loves us that much.

And what I truly cherish is this: today's verse is from a book of the Bible written some seven hundred years before Christ's birth. Yet my sins—which break my heart and His—are "blotted out" today and every day, even though God has it within His infinite power to rewind and recollect them without a moment's effort. How?

Someone walks between God and me in order to block what God prefers to forget. Someone sacrificed everything so His Father would always see the best in me. ⟶ Trish

TODAY'S PRAYER
. . . .

Gracious Father, Your grace is so hard to fathom—
that You would choose to forgive my sins against You.
Even harder to fathom is the way You and Your precious Son
have chosen to block my sins from Your view forever.
I pray for a constant indwelling of the Holy Spirit
to help me avoid adding to the transgressions
You choose to ignore. I love You.

Gloriously Inefficient

*The LORD will vindicate me; your love, LORD, endures forever—
do not abandon the works of your hands.*

PSALM 138:8

I could have been an efficiency expert. I dislike grocery shopping because of the inefficiency of it. Pick an item off the shelf and put it into the grocery cart. Lift same item—and a hundred of its cousins—out of the cart and onto the checkout conveyor belt. Load them from the conveyor into bags and into the cart again. Already, the redundancy appalls me. Push the cart across the parking lot and unload those same groceries to the trunk of the car. Once home, haul those miserable bags of tonnage into the house, unpack each of the bags, and handle those grocery items yet again to find them spots in the cupboard, fridge, or freezer.

In what factory would that plan pass inspection? Any efficiency expert worth her clipboard would suggest that handling an item so many times is the height of *dummkopf*ness.

That may be why my husband's idea of an ideal vacation gets check marks in the "You're Kidding, Right?" column on my clipboard. Oh, the inefficiency! Collect a bunch of fishing and canoeing equipment for weeks in the garage and a corner of my dining room (yes, ladies), cram it all into the truck, strap a canoe on top so you'll have a nice, high-pitched whistling sound to accompany the trip, drive forever past some perfectly good lakes and rivers until you get to the "right" one, pile the equipment into the canoe, paddle until just this side of the edge of the earth, unload the canoe, haul the equipment up Extreme Sports cliff faces to a relatively flat piece of granite, set up camp, sleep a minute, tear down camp, load it all into the canoe—and you see my point.

Even the grunts in a tennis match seem an energy drain my birthing coach would nix. I load the dishwasher while talking on the phone. I clean the top of the washing machine while filling it. I don't buy shirts that need ironing…or that might *potentially* need ironing if, say, left in the dryer too long. I don't like single-function kitchen tools. If it can't do more than one thing, it doesn't stay. Efficiency is the key.

Or is it?

It's hard to listen when efficiency is the goal. Compassion and efficiency don't mix well; compassion takes time. Grace sometimes requires excess movement—leaning in farther than halfway, stepping around piles of regret, dropping every other important responsibility to attend to the messy need of a human heart…

How many times have I missed a moment when the Lord's purpose for me was to make me gloriously inefficient? Cynthia

TODAY'S PRAYER

Lord of all, my drive for efficiency can interfere with Your purposes for me. I mourn the repetitiveness of a full grocery cart and neglect the emptiness in the eyes of the clerk. I put off a joy moment with a friend until it fits into a more efficient spot in my schedule. I slot time alone with You for when I know I'll be waiting anyway…and I can't believe I just admitted that to You. Forgive me. Make me gloriously inefficient when that better serves Your purposes for me.

Purified and Sanctified

He will sit as a refiner and purifier of silver.

MALACHI 3:3

One afternoon, while chatting with a dear friend and catching up on one another's lives, I told her about a time-sensitive blessing I'd been praying about for months. As the deadline grew closer, I'd begun to lose faith, and I asked her for prayer coverage as I awaited an answer to my dilemma.

"Of course I'll pray for you," she promised. "But this is always the way God deals with you, Sandie. You're that person who makes it all the way to the scary cliff, teetering right on the edge, and that's when God snatches you to safety and provides just what you need. He never seems to show up for you any sooner than absolutely necessary."

That observation really stuck with me. Was that really how the Lord chose to deal with me? I went over the last few challenges I'd faced in my life, the really big ones where I'd prayed and prayed for an answer and—*what do you know!*—that's exactly what had happened.

In the book of Malachi, we're told that God presides over us as a refiner, in much the same way that silver is purified. That connection really makes me think about the way my life unfolds during those times that I find myself questioning whether or not God might have forgotten about me.

The silversmith heats a piece of silver over the hottest part of the fire for however long it takes for the impurities to melt away. If God "sits as a refiner," does this mean that He sits there with us when we're in the hot seat, watching over us to make sure we're not there any longer than we need to be? And what happens if we are?

If the silversmith holds the precious metal over the flames too long, the silver is destroyed. His full attention is required at all times to make sure that the purifying process is thorough but that the silver is removed from the heat when it needs to be.

The vision of my Father as the silversmith, refining and improving me, is a new joy in my life that I carry with me. I refer to that mental picture all the time: He tenderly holds me over the fire, cautious not to let me fall when the heat of the battle intensifies, paying close attention to the specific impurities that need to be eliminated. At that precise moment when I've taken all I can and the fire has done its work in me, He pulls me away from the flames and looks me over. If I'm pure and clean in that one area, shiny enough to reflect His image, there is (for the moment, at least) blessed relief. With each new purification by fire, I am another step closer to ultimate perfection in Christ Jesus.

How many times have *you* looked into the fire and forgotten that the silversmith had you well in hand? ⸺ Sandie

TODAY'S PRAYER

Father God, help me to remain steady in Your hand,
even if it takes me into the fire for a moment or two.
Your care is all-inclusive, and I know
You'll never let me endure more than I'm able.

Rooks, Pawns, and Faithful Moves

Trust in him at all times, you people;
pour out your hearts to him, for God is our refuge.

PSALM 62:8

My widowed cousin put her faith in a dating service, and her daughter met the love of her life on Myspace. A couple at our church relied on a Korean-based agency to match them with a beautiful daughter, and a friend believed his Russian bride would be everything the brochure promised.

Me? I don't even trust the *word* "trust!" And why would I, when one minute it's a verb ("Trust me, I'll pay back every penny of that loan!"); and in the next, it's a noun ("Free toaster for opening an account!"). Translated from ancient Norse, *traust* equals comfort. Really? I should feel comfortable relying on this thing that can't decide what it is?

I needn't be a chess champion to understand that I need to look four to six moves ahead or prepare to hear, "Checkmate!" When the weatherman predicts a blizzard, I stock up on milk and toilet paper. Uncle Joe's coming? Better hide the beer. I'm "insurance poor," thanks to auto/house/health/life policies, and I print MapQuest directions before leaving on a car trip.

Lack of trust in things and people is what makes me plan for every eventuality. So it always surprises unbelievers to hear that my heart overflows with hope. They don't understand that trust and faith are very different entities—or that my faith stems from belief in a merciful Father who promises that if I put my trust in *Him*, He will be my protection, my refuge, my strength.

When unbelievers ask how I can accept on faith that God will deliver on His promises, I say faith in God is easy! It doesn't require plans. Or maps. Or thinking four to six moves ahead. Putting my trust in the people and things of the world isn't anywhere near as easy as putting my faith in the Lord!

Speaking of easy, my church friends are finding it easy to love their raven-haired daughter. My cousin's easy-to-love beau is a "keeper." Sadly, things aren't easy for the guy whose mail-order bride emptied his bank account and disappeared. And my cousin's daughter didn't have an easy time reading about her dreamboat's new girlfriend…on his Myspace page.

In the park last week, I saw two elderly gents hunched over a chessboard. "If you learn well the meaning of trust," said one as he nabbed the black knight, "others will give you the earth."

His friend toppled the white queen and snorted, "But betray them, and they'll hunt you to the ends of the earth."

What a blessing that, as Christians, we only need to look *one* move ahead and place our trust in the Almighty! Loree

TODAY'S PRAYER

I come to You, Father, humbled by the depth of Your love.
Long before I drew my first breath, Your promise of protection
surrounded me, and there it will remain until my last breath is
spent, though nothing I might do in the in-between time
will make me worthy of it. If ever I should be so foolish
as to step outside the safety of that loving grace,
I pray You'll cast Your net and draw me close again!

Kids! I'm Tellin' Ya!

*"I will heal their waywardness and love them freely,
for my anger has turned away from them."*

HOSEA 14:4

My adult daughter is a phenomenal person. She's smart, savvy, and a can-do girl. She's thoroughly reliable and straight-shooting.

But as a teenager? Not so much. She was such an obedient baby and child but, mercy, things sure changed after that.

I gave birth to her brother when she turned fourteen. So she hit her teen years with a new sibling, far less attention than Mom had ever given her before, a fairly new stepfather, a new hometown, a new school, and the task of making all new friends. She had a lot to tackle, and having her hormones kick in certainly didn't add stability to the equation.

So we had a few rough years there, during which I was constantly disciplining her. And no matter how badly she had behaved, no matter how often I caught her in a lie or skipping school or "partying," no matter how upset or angry I got with her, I hated having to punish her. It was the only part of parenting I remember with sadness. But not regret.

As an adult, my daughter often laughs about what a pain in the neck she was, how bad she was. I'm able to laugh about it, too, now that it's all over and we're fabulous friends.

Now, my son was a different story. His first three years just about killed me. He was a powerful little cuss, and he quickly developed unshakable opinions about what he wanted. He was never one of those kids you could distract from the light socket with a jingly toy monkey. And tantrums? He made the Tasmanian Devil look like a *puddy tat*. So we had our rough years early, and I had to do a major upgrade on my early-learning discipline practices.

It just so happened, if you haven't yet done the math, that both my kids had their "rough" patches at the very same time in my life. So Mom was taxed to the max.

Yet when my son hit four, he started to change. He had actually accepted the Lord at three—as well as a three-year-old can—and he became the sweetest kid ever. We soon learned he was extremely smart, he had a strong moral core, and he was absolutely loving and lovable. He's now in college, and he's remained that same terrific kid, even throughout his teenage years. I honestly don't think I've had to discipline him since he was three.

Those few years during which my teenaged daughter and toddler son seemed to have conspired to drive me insane brought out the worst in me. I was worn-out, short on patience, and often angry. But I was never out of love with my challenging kids. As most parents would say, I would have fought a grizzly bear for either one of them.

No doubt I've put God in this same position. He's probably been angry and had to discipline me, but I know He's always turned his anger away from me eventually. As a parent, I understand that. As His child, I am ever thankful for it. ⌐ Trish

TODAY'S PRAYER

Dearest Lord, thank You for Your discipline.
And thank You for Your constant, unwavering love.

Shelter

The name of the LORD is a fortified tower;
the righteous run to it and are safe.

PROVERBS 18:10

I wonder if the cops would find my fingerprints on the remote control. Not that there'd be any reason for law enforcement to dust it for fingerprints. My prints are all over the washing machine knobs, the dryer controls, the dishwasher handle, the broom handle, the vacuum cleaner, the phone, the computer keyboard…

The television remote?

As in many households, the remote is more my husband's area of expertise.

We don't agree on much when it comes to television viewing. The incessant blare of a basketball game between two teams I've never heard of can send me into an emotional seizure. The droning monotone of the History Channel puts me into a temporary coma. For some reason, reruns—of almost anything—feel like chewing yesterday's gum. Maybe it's a phase I'm going through.

But my husband and I do agree on one type of show—survival shows, especially the non-Hollywood kind. We're fascinated by people who find ingenious ways of surviving being stranded in the Alaskan wilderness or on a remote Indonesian island or in a desert, on a glacier, in an untamed jungle…

From our overstuffed chairs, we coach the survivors.

"See those cattails? You can use the fluff inside to start a fire. You need fire."

"Don't drink that pond scum. I don't care how thirsty you are, you'll be sorry if you—Oh, man!"

"If you don't lash that bamboo raft tighter, when you hit the rapids it'll— Told you so."

"What do you mean, you have nothing to eat? Can't anyone figure out how to catch fish?" (That, from my husband, the fisherman.)

We're in awe of those who face their fears and rappel down the cliff face, who endure one miserable night after another, who pull something meaningful out of the debris washed up by a storm or out of the depths of their character.

As we look around at our neighbors and church family, we feel the same sense of awe. The couple facing their medical fears, lowering themselves over the cliff face anyway. The caregiver enduring one miserable night after another. The young man picking through the driftwood of his life, finding a little something he can use.

On the televised survival shows, the inexperienced, uneducated, or unwilling-to-learn leave shelter-building for last, after they've tanned or napped or looked for pretty seashells. The same is true in life, I guess.

Two palm fronds and a stick? You call that a shelter? Let me show you the Fortress I run to for shelter, the impenetrable Refuge, the strong and unbreakable Tower the team (Father, Son, and Holy Spirit) provides for me. It won't collapse in the middle of the night. Hurricane winds can't topple it. Earthquakes can't rattle it. Impeccable design. And it's portable. It goes where I go. ⇝ Cynthia

TODAY'S PRAYER
· · · · · · · · · · · · · · · · · · · ·

Father God, it's time I expressed more gratitude
for the shelter You've provided. It's helped me to survive
when I thought I couldn't. Too often I'm peering out the
window, shaken by the sight of the storm forming,
when I should be tapping on the walls to reassure
my heart of the unfailing stability of my Refuge.

Who Is Your Barnabas?

But Barnabas took him and brought him to the apostles.
He told them how Saul on his journey had seen the Lord
and that the Lord had spoken to him, and how in Damascus
he had preached fearlessly in the name of Jesus.

ACTS 9:27

Last year, I wrote a blog post based on the realization that we all have a Barnabas or two in our lives—someone who steps up for the sole purpose of our advancement rather than their own. I received more e-mail about that one post than all the others from the previous month combined.

There's something that happens when we use our spiritual eyes to look into the distance rather than focus only on our own limited sphere. I like to call my sphere SandieLand. It's that place where everything revolves around ME, and anything else that affects ME is just secondary to—you guessed it!—ME. SandieLand can be a funny little place where perspective is skewed and wise decisions are seldom made. In SandieLand, I'm epic, a legend! In my own mind. But out there in the real world…not so much.

Paul started out as a pretty bad dude. Known as Saul of Tarsus, he devoted himself to the persecution of Christ's disciples. Then one day, walking along the road and minding his own business, probably lost in thought about how to make life miserable for those ignorant Christians, the Lord appeared to him in a flood of light. It was so profound that Paul was actually blinded for a few days from it, but when his sight came around again, he was a believer. A dramatic salvation experience is life-changing! I'm reminded of my own born-again experience and the stunned reaction of my Hollywood friends when I suddenly became a very different person.

I doubt anyone would have given Paul's Christian influence the time of day if not for Barnabas staking his reputation and standing up to tell people, "Look, this guy was just in Damascus boldly preaching about Jesus Christ. I'm telling you, he's for real!"

I've had a few people like Barnabas in my life, people who helped to pave the road intended for me. I know that every one of them was a gift of grace from God, and I'm convinced that Barnabas was anointed with that same kind of mission to set the stage for Paul's sharing the Good News throughout history in his preaching as well as his New Testament writings.

Would Paul have served God without Barnabas? Almost certainly. God's grace provides answers and avenues in places where they didn't previously exist, and He inspires others to take a stand and offer a leg up for those who can't do it for themselves.

Is there a Barnabas in your life that you haven't stopped to thank? I encourage you to do that—sooner rather than later. But more importantly…how can you deliver the grace of Barnabas into someone else's life? ⌣ Sandie

TODAY'S PRAYER
. . . .

Lord Jesus, thank You for the detailed, intricate role You play in our journeys. Thank You for the people You bring across our paths when we need a Barnabas the most. Please anoint me to pay it forward into the lives of others.

When Friendship Hurts

Say to wisdom, "You are my sister,"
and to insight, "You are my relative."
PROVERBS 7:4

When someone says, "Hey, Loree, I'd like you to meet So-and-so," what am I to do, hand out an "Are you trustworthy?" questionnaire and keep my distance until she fills it out? I prefer to give her my hand and leave the "Is she trustworthy?" part to God.

The trouble is, I don't always remember to ask for His guidance. And even when I do, I'm not always good at reading His answers.

Take, for example, a woman I met years ago, when she and her husband were newcomers to our church. Married and a stay-at-home mom, she also hoped someday to see her words in print. With all we had in common, this budding friendship seemed too good to be true. As we swapped recipes and sipped herbal tea while our children romped in her backyard or mine, it never crossed my mind to ask what *God* thought of the relationship.

In the coming year, He blessed me with articles and short stories that appeared in newspapers and magazines. I took a one-night-a-week job, teaching "Writing and Marketing Freelance Articles" at the community college…step one in realizing my dream of having a novel published.

Meanwhile, my friend self-published her own novel, and I was proud to agree when she asked for my help in marketing it. Then, she came to me for a recommendation and guidance so that she, too, could teach at the college, and I gave it…all without first asking for the *Father's* guidance.

Not long afterward, as I recovered from a serious illness, my friend came to visit with a box of candies in one hand and a stack of papers in the other. If I hadn't read her ad in the local paper the following week, I might never have known that, while borrowing my copy machine, she'd also "borrowed" class and workshop notes, lesson plans, and my business proposal for an in-house writers' studio.

Deeply hurt and disappointed, I took the heartache—finally— to the Lord, and He provided still more evidence that it's never too late to bring my problems, however big or small, to His throne.

If I'd gone to Him sooner, might I have spared myself this sadness? Absolutely!

But just as my earthly father ran alongside me, holding the seat as I learned to ride my two-wheeler, my heavenly Father knew that the only way I'd figure out the delicate balance between trust and true friendship was if He let go and let me fall.

In the following months, my friend quietly faded from my life. Too busy running her writers' studio to find time to call or visit? Perhaps. I prefer to think that *she* gained something from the experience too.

 Loree

TODAY'S PRAYER
. . . .

Dear Father, I have not earned a single one of Your gifts—
not even the freedom to call on Your divine guidance
as I choose friends and associates who will echo
Your presence in my life. Thank You for providing me
with the will to be a good friend, to stay a safe distance
from those who are not...and the wisdom
to know one from the other.

Always Appreciated

Come and see what God has done,
his awesome deeds for mankind!

PSALM 66:5

My Mr.-Magoo-like eyesight has been one of my more notorious physical characteristics throughout life.

Two years before the 1966 rubella vaccine was discovered, I was struck during the pandemic that swept Europe and the U.S. There were other children and infants who fared worse than me, losing their hearing, sight, mental faculties, even their lives. I returned to school unaware that my eyes had been affected. I was a good reader before I got sick, but suddenly I couldn't grasp the words on the board. My teacher could tell—I was squinting—and off to the clinic she sent me.

All these years I've worn goofy glasses and hard contact lenses (which I chased across windy school yards or frantically hunted on disco dance floors). I've fallen asleep wearing my lenses and awoken with scratched corneas and eye infections. At forty-something, I started wearing reading glasses on top of the contacts—and there's just something wrong with that picture.

I've always craved LASIK surgery, but it seemed right up there, luxury-wise, with designer purses, Brazilian blowouts, and annual jaunts to the Caribbean. Still, the lure of fuss-free vision prompted a saving frenzy. Once I felt flush enough to pay for the surgery, I took the plunge. I finally had it done last year, and I love the results.

Still, I've already become so used to seeing without glasses that sometimes I take it for granted. I got out of the shower the other day and was reminded of how fantastic it was to see everything around me clearly and comfortably. As I've done ever since the surgery, I stopped to thank God for the gift of my corrected vision.

I know what terrible vision is like, so I have a greater appreciation for my new clarity. Similarly, people who live with physical challenges—the inability to hear, walk, go through a day without pain—know by contrast how much better their lives could be. Nevertheless, we're *all* blessed by "what God has done."

Sometimes I catch myself subtly moping about the disappointments of my day. I get out of bed dreading some task I have to do that day, or I go to bed aware of something that didn't pan out the way I had hoped. *Why not, Lord? Why me, God?* I can even stretch that dissatisfaction to cover the responsibilities and results of the past week. Or month. Or year.

How much better my days would seem if I started and ended them by considering how my body—even this imperfect one—is blessed. How much brighter my outlook would be if I considered how He protects my loved ones and my friends. How much more content I'd be if each night I took the time to appreciate my comfortable bed…food in the pantry…freedom to worship…the vast, beautiful skies…the smallest hummingbird…the warm sun…the cool breeze. The many gorgeous vistas here and abroad. Music. Laughter. Breath. My heartbeat.

Salvation.

Oh, come and see what our God has done! There is so much to appreciate. ～ Trish

TODAY'S PRAYER

Gracious Father, Your never-ending love for us is so abundant
and complete that we struggle to fathom it. Thank You
for Your generous patience when we take for granted
Your awesome works on our behalf.

Gold Rush

Gold there is, and rubies in abundance
but lips that speak knowledge are a rare jewel.
PROVERBS 20:15

Jesus never said anything dumb.

Can you imagine never having to apologize for something you said? Never suffering embarrassment over calling your insurance agent's wife by another name? No string of unsightly "ums" in a job interview or speaking gig? Imagine a relationship with no "Sorry, that's not what I meant." How much more sleep might I have enjoyed if my mind hadn't replayed the missteps my mouth made earlier that day? Can you imagine the relief of knowing that every word spoken was golden?

My husband was enamored with the televised real-life drama of a team of rookie gold miners who left their homes and families with one purpose—to strike it rich with Alaskan gold. The team had aging, cobbled equipment and just enough knowledge to be dangerous. Propelled by a series of calamities a fiction editor would have declared too numerous to be believed, the men scraped and pitted and pockmarked the Alaskan wilderness in search of golden treasure.

They panned by hand and processed rocks and soil with nerve-rattling giant machinery. Nothing. They collected buckets of black sand that held the promise of gold flakes. Nothing. They stayed up all night pumping water out of caverns they'd created, looking for a long-buried and long-silent waterfall with an elusive pot of gold at its base.

The men spent all they had and kept spending, ignoring their overdue mortgages and the bill collectors at their doors back home because of the lure of gold.

A mountain of discarded dirt and gold-less rocks, injuries, illness, and broken relationships stood as testaments to the draw of a precious metal so valuable a medicine bottle full could buy a car.

The men burned through tankers full of fuel and truckloads of food and all their reserves of patience. The summer they thought would net them a fortune turned into snow and bone-chilling temperatures that threatened their chances to recover even the cost of the Bengay they'd used on screaming muscles.

Then, finally, there it was. A nugget. And another. Not enough to get them out of financial trouble, but enough to feed their frenzy for more.

Months of work and sacrifice. Monumental expenditures of everything worth spending in pursuit of something they deemed worth saving.

And God says, by comparison, that gold is plentiful. What He considers rare are lips that speak true knowledge.

What if I looked at my opinions as if they were pyrite—fool's gold—and at genuine knowledge as genuine gold? How many words could I pan out of my day? How many conversations would I discard, dross not worth saving? What if I spoke, Tweeted, Facebooked, and wrote only words that mattered?

What if I moved so closely in tune with the Spirit of God that I could have the same confidence Jesus did—with no dumb words?

Imagine. ⌐ Cynthia

TODAY'S PRAYER
· · · · · · · · · · · · · · · · · · · ·

Lord, when I think of how many words I've wasted and
how few have been meaningful, helpful, or golden, it makes
me wish I had a bulldozer large enough to scoop up the dross
and haul it away. Thank You for Your amazing grace that
gets excited about a nugget from me here and there.

Supply and Demand

As far as the east is from the west,
so far has he removed our transgressions from us.

PSALM 103:12

Have you ever tried to explain the grace of God to someone? It's one of the most beautiful and humbling blessings in our lives—that amazing promise that nothing can separate us from the love and forgiveness of our God—and yet the concept is so hard for some people to wrap their brains around. It's not even a case of supply and demand, is it? How do we tell them there's not only enough but also an abundance available, *beyond* what we need?

I have one particular friend who just can't get past this one issue in her spiritual journey.

"You mean to tell me," she recapped after a particularly long conversation about my beliefs, "some guy can go out and torture and murder someone and live a completely worthless life, but on his death-bed, he can just say, 'Oops, sorry!' and he's forgiven everything? That guy should be punished, not find some touchy-feely forgiveness."

"Well," I replied thoughtfully, praying to find the right words, "it's not exactly that simple. He can't just *say it*. Forgiveness is about far more than a couple of words; it's about the thoughts and intents of the heart. He has to really *mean it*, have true remorse."

"Well, how are you going to know if he means it or not?"

"It doesn't matter if I think he does. God knows whether he's sincere, and He's the one who ultimately judges us all."

We went back and forth like that for an hour, looking at hypothetical murderers and rapists and con men, every one of whom my friend used as an effective barrier between herself and God. It kind of broke my heart, really, because she's one of the sweetest people I've ever met, and I want so much to hang out with her in eternity.

I've often looked back at the conversation, wondering if there was something else I could have said, some genius way I might have explained the loving grace of God so that she might have looked past the murderer in her imagination who clearly didn't deserve a place in heaven. Another criminal comes to mind when I remember that exchange, the one who turned to the Man hanging on the cross beside him to ask that he be remembered when Jesus reached His kingdom. And so every time I pray for my treasured friend now, I ask the Lord to lead her to that kind of grace. Even if she rebels until the very last minute of her life, I pray that she will turn to Him in search of salvation so we can share the joy that comes after this life. ⟶ Sandie

TODAY'S PRAYER

Lord Jesus, may we always carry the beauty and grace found at the cross in our hearts and minds. Help me to live my life in a way that is not only pleasing to You but that will also reflect Your love and salvation to the people You put into my life. In and of myself, I'm so sadly lacking, Father. But through Your Spirit, equip me to show the people around me that road that leads straight to You.

The Prayer Wars

*Give thanks in all circumstances;
for this is for this is God's will for you in Christ Jesus.*
1 THESSALONIANS 5:18

My grandkids love to say grace.

Not the rote "God Is Great, God Is Good" poem we're all familiar with, but something pure and simple and straight from the heart, because that's how they've been taught to pray. Suffice it to say, Sunday dinners at my house are interesting. And the food is usually cold by the time the blessing ends, because the word "simple" to my grandkids has no connection to the word "brief!" Last week, for example, my granddaughter decided we should all take turns saying a blessing.

"But it isn't even Thanksgiving," said her twin, Steven.

"Just because it isn't Thanksgiving doesn't mean we can't say thanks," Samantha shot back.

"Well, all right," he agreed, "but you have to start." He pointed to his grandfather, who sat on Sam's left. "And go *that way* around the table."

Her head bobbed as she did a mental head count, and she whispered, "Twelve whole prayers! God is gonna *love* this!" Smiling, she bowed her head, folded her hands, and opened with, "Dear Lord, we thank You for all this food and for making the seeds, and for the men and women who grew them into plants and the truck drivers who delivered the plants to the Super-Fresh." She opened one eye and whispered, "Granddad, your turn."

"We thank You for our good health and our homes, and—"

"—and Grandmom," Steven chimed in, "who cooked all of this *and* set the table *and* made chocolate cake."

"Hey, it wasn't your turn," pretty Payton said, before adding, "Thank

You, dear God, that I got five gold stars last week. And that Emily's pinkeye is all better. *And* that Mr. Arnold's puppy didn't get runned over when it runned into the street."

"And that baby Warner's poopy diaper didn't leak on his crib," Steven said.

"Steven!" Samantha said with a gasp. "You can't say 'poopy' in a *prayer*!"

He faced Samantha. "Why not? God made people, and people poop!"

Shoulders slumped, she groaned and shook her head as baby Warner said, "Poop!"

"Boys," Samantha groaned. Then, "Please God, let the soldiers all stay safe, and don't let their children miss them too much until they get home. And send lots of food and clean water to the hurricane people."

"Yes, yes!" Payton squealed, "And clothes and blankets for the children, and flashlights so they won't be a-scared when it gets dark out."

Meeting with God in this way recharges my batteries; what He does through each of us, by faith as we receive His grace, has eternity stamped on it.

Since my own childhood, I've held fast to Jesus' words: "I [have] come that they might have life, and that they might have it more abundantly" (John 10:10 KJV). I searched the faces of loved ones seated around the table—the adults stifling chuckles as the children continued to pray—and wondered, could life *get* any more grace-filled than this? Loree

TODAY'S PRAYER

Lord, though our world is rife with sin and suffering, You help us
to recognize the blessings that You deliver. Let me say
thank You, daily, with the pure, sweet sincerity of a child.

Too Successful
for Your Own Good

"I praise you, Father, Lord of heaven and earth,
because you have hidden these things from the wise and learned,
and revealed them to little children."

LUKE 10:21

Here's a pop quiz for you. What do these people have in common?

- Industrialist/businessman/philanthropist Andrew Carnegie (of Carnegie Hall fame).
- Physiologist/psychologist/physician Ivan Pavlov (of Pavlovian-dog fame).
- Actress Katharine Hepburn (winner of four Academy Awards).
- American investor/philanthropist Warren Buffet (the richest man in the world in 2008).
- Chinese martial artist Bruce Lee (undisputed king of martial arts).
- Rock-and-roll legend Mick Jagger (ancient—but still kicking—rocker).
- Facebook developer Mark Zuckerberg (one of *Time* magazine's Most Influential People of 2008).

Yes, they all are (or were) famous. All successful in their fields. All brilliant in their own areas of expertise.

And all self-professed atheists.

Now, there's not a dummy in the bunch. They were each blessed with some extraordinary talent. But, apparently, none of them recognized (or recognizes) his or her blessings as *blessings*. Surely they recognized that they were gifted, but they credited themselves or past mentors or hard knocks with getting them where they got to be.

That's beyond sad. These people weren't pygmies in some remote jungle. No doubt every one of them went around the block often enough to have heard the gospel message at least once. Each of them emphatically responded, "Thanks, but no thanks."

Jesus spoke today's verse when some of his disciples came back to Him after telling others the same thing John the Baptist did: "Prepare the way for the Lord" (Mark 1:3). "The kingdom of God has come near to you" (Luke 10:9). (And was He ever!) While many people repented of their sins and turned to God, many others didn't. Jesus thanked His Father for withholding the truth from those who considered themselves far too "wise and learned" to submit to God. And He thanked God for those so willing to humble themselves to God that they were like children.

Anyone who has that deep, abiding relationship with Christ knows what Jesus was talking about. Every one of us was told, at some point in our lives, that God lives, that we were created in His image but were separated from His perfect holiness because of sin. We were each told that Christ died in our place—He took on the punishment we had coming for our sins. And we were told that we simply needed to recognize ourselves as sinners who needed that sacrifice on His part, to accept that fact and to accept His amazing, loving gesture for what it was. Unconditional love. Salvation. Redemption. The only way.

One needn't really know or understand *anything* else to be considered blameless in God's eyes. You don't need to get a degree in apologetics or become a biblical scholar (or any kind of scholar, for that matter).

Christ's gracious choice to make that humble sacrifice and our choice to come to Him like children both boil down to the same condition of the heart. And it's not wisdom. It's not accomplishment. It's not learning. It's acceptance. ⌒ Trish

TODAY'S PRAYER
. . . .

Precious Jesus, thank You for Your humility in taking my place
of suffering. I pray You will help me represent that same
humility and draw the "wise" and "learned" closer to You.

Slower Now

The LORD is gracious and compassionate,
slow to anger and rich in love.

PSALM 145:8

My daughter Amy called to say she was sorry. Again.

In true déjà-vu style, her kindergartner unintentionally reenacted a scene at school so reminiscent of something Amy did thirty years ago that little Hannah could have served detention for copycatting as well as for disregarding the playground rules.

Detention. Kindergarten. What's wrong with this picture?

Fresh from her own daughter's remorse, my firstborn apologized for an offense thirty years old because she saw it reenacted in her child. Her apology made me laugh. What goes around comes around, as they say.

I'd always resisted the threat some parents hurl at their kids: "I hope you have a child just like you!" I wish I could spare my daughter from parental angst, from embarrassment and concern and frustration. But you have to admit it's kind of funny when detention history repeats itself.

Wisdom and love tell me to pray for my grandkids and for the amazing people who parent them. Detention's no laughing matter if it doesn't lead to a change in behavior.

Where have I heard that before?

I'm slower than I used to be. When Amy and her two brothers put snow down a schoolmate's neck or pulled a zero on their homework because they forgot to turn it in <sigh>, I reacted with one of several instant Mom Responses as if the message were already written and all I had to do was hit "SEND."

"…living up to your potential…" "…responsibility…" "…respect authority…" "Be ye kind one to another…or else!"

The fine line between frustration and anger wavered like the horizontal hold on a 1950s television screen. (I saw one once at the Smithsonian. And, okay, in my family's living room.)

Today, when my grandchildren misbehave, I have to concentrate to keep from chuckling. When one of them tried to flush a handful of golf balls, a manila folder, and a paintbrush, I—the person who didn't have to tear into the plumbing project—thought it was creative. When another, at little more than a year old, stacked pillows to form a staircase to help him reach something he found intriguing, I snatched him to safety, restarted my heart, and said, "The boy's going to make a fine engineer." When his brother played stylist and gave them both inventive haircuts, my first response was to take pictures.

Another grandson perfected melodrama before he turned two, dropping his chin to his chest and slumping his shoulders to register life-altering heartbreak. Anything could trigger the toddler version of a broken heart.

"No, you can't have another snack right now." "Sorry, but you have to wear socks with those shoes." "Honey, it's raining."

Adorable, right?

The Lord doesn't find my misbehavior cute—that unkind word, impatience with my husband, avoidance of what I know He wants me to do. He doesn't chuckle at my melodrama or comment that my attempt to manufacture an answer to prayer shows my engineering skills.

But where would I be if He weren't slow to anger and rich in love?

— Cynthia

TODAY'S PRAYER

· · · · · · · · · · · · · · · · · · ·

Father God, thank You for loving me through my tantrums,
my rants, my detention-worthy moments that would
try anyone's grace but Yours.

From the Mouths of Babes

But by the grace of God I am what I am,
and his grace to me was not without effect.

1 CORINTHIANS 15:10

I lived in a Los Angeles suburb at the time, working as the director of the children's ministry at my home church while studying my writing craft. I had a very happy life…and then a big shoe dropped on me out of nowhere. I'd been deeply betrayed by someone I never could have imagined capable of such a thing. I was devastated.

While on nursery duty with a close friend one Sunday morning, I rocked a sleeping baby in my arms as she changed the diaper of another while we chatted. "I'm absolutely destroyed," I confided. "I can't even think clearly about where to go from here. The situation is overwhelming, and it's just too big out there in front of me."

"What's too big, Miss Sandie?"

One of my special, favorite five-year-olds had wandered in from the classroom next door.

"Oh, I'm just working through some grown-up problems," I told him. "And until I figure things out, they just look really big to me. Does that make sense?"

His little brow furrowed, and he thought it over with deep intensity before he finally nodded. "I guess so," he replied. "Can I help?"

"Nope," I said as I smiled at him. "You go on over and finish craft time now, okay?"

He nodded and obediently opened the door to his classroom and stepped inside.

About an hour later, after the last baby had been picked up from the nursery, I stood at the sink washing pacifiers, and that same little boy walked up behind me and tapped my arm. "Hey, Miss Sandie, look through my spyglass," he said softly, and he held up a small plastic telescope. But he lifted it toward my face by the wrong end.

"I think it goes the other way," I instructed. But when I tried to turn it around, he resisted.

"No," he cried. "If you look through this end, everything in front of you looks smaller. Remember when you said it was too big in front of you? Through this end, it won't seem so big."

When the depth of what that little five-year-old boy told me began to sink in, I tried to hold back the tears, but they spilled out anyway.

"You know what," I said to him. "You just reminded me of something I already should have known. Your spyglass shows me how I see things from one end and how God sees the same things from the other one. I think you might be some kind of boy genius!"

He burst into laughter at that, and it sounded a lot like music to me. Before I knew it, my heart was lighter and I laughed with him.

Many times over the years that have followed that Sunday morning, I've calmed myself by remembering to "turn the telescope around" for a fresh look at my life from a different perspective. ⁓ Sandie

TODAY'S PRAYER
· · · · · · · · · · · · · · · · · · · ·

Thank You, Father, for the grace and wisdom of a simple,
childlike view of faith. Help me not to complicate things
so much by meditating on them. Instead, help me to set them
down at Your feet with the faith of a little child.

Yes, Virginia, There Is Grace in Silly Putty!

A gossip betrays a confidence, but a trustworthy person keeps a secret.
PROVERBS 11:13

Whether we realize it or not, every mother is blessed with *acting talent*. As proof, let me tell you about one sunny Saturday afternoon from my past:

"Oh, Timmy was no trouble, no trouble at all!" the birthday boy's mom said, smiling like a pageant winner when the little monster's dad came to fetch him. (I'd worn that all-teeth, no-truth smile enough times to recognize artificial sweetener when I saw it.)

When my own all-in-pink cutie-pie asked if I could make the six helium balloons tied to her wrist fit into the backseat with her little sister, the dog, the baby's car seat *and* the diaper bag, I said, "Are you kidding? Mommies can do *any*thing!" Experience taught me that the bobbing inflatables would render the rearview mirror useless, but I'd survived many a white-knuckled drive home from clown-and-cake shindigs…

Arriving home, my li'l darling scattered the contents of her goodie bag across the kitchen table, and a colorful plastic egg rolled out. I nearly ground my molars to dust, hiding my disdain; what kind of fiend subjects another mother to the evils of Silly Putty? While immersing the party dress into a tub of clean-and-soak, I hid another scowl. Who serves grape juice at a kids' party?

The kind who leaves her husband for an old high-school sweetheart—if the rumors in the car-pool lane were true.

My best friend's daughter had attended the party too; commiseration was sure to keep my well-acted "I'm okay, you're okay" grin in place until sweetie pie's sugar high wore off. I reached for the phone…but something stopped me.

Ancient Chinese proverbs and childlike slurs echoed in my head (things like, "If you control your tongue, you will master your life" and "What you say bounces off me and sticks to you"). Gossip, I'd learned, can turn an innocent lump of Silly Putty into the ominous ball of tar that costarred with Steve McQueen in *The Blob*.

I remembered, too, a Bible study where my pastor criticized the church for being the only army that kills its wounded; he'd counseled troubled sisters in faith who, instead of receiving the love and encouragement of fellow Christians, had felt the slice of sharp tongues.

I grabbed the Good Book, and God led me to Proverbs 26:22. Red-faced with shame, I opened the plastic egg, pressed the blob briefly to that gilded page, then carefully rolled it up and stored it in its colorful container.

Now, whenever I'm tempted to participate in gossip, I *un*roll it and read, "The words of a gossip are like choice morsels; they go down to the inmost parts"…all while "acting" as though I'd only hidden the egg to protect my carpets and upholstery from the destructive powers of Silly Putty.

Loree

TODAY'S PRAYER

O Father, forgive me for every human frailty that I've yet
to overcome. Bless me with the wisdom to notice and turn
away from gossip and gossipers. Give me the right words
to comfort those harmed by hurtful words and the strength
to remind those who speak them that without fuel,
that hurtful and ungraceful fire will suffocate!

Why Me, Lord?

He chose David his servant and took him from the sheep pens;
from tending the sheep he brought him to be the shepherd
of his people Jacob, of Israel his inheritance.

PSALM 78:70–71

What's my *purpose?*

We all wonder that at some point, right? Entire mega enterprises have been built around our innate desire to understand why, specifically, God put each of us here on earth. As Christians eager to show our appreciation for Christ's gift of salvation, we're particularly keen to know how we can live our lives according to His plan. We all wonder, *Why am I here?*

Some people have clearly been chosen to be Christian leaders— pastors, worship leaders, Bible study leaders, Sunday school teachers. They usually know they've been chosen because they *enjoy* what they're doing. Yes, some people perform these tasks out of a sense of obligation, but others experience God-given peace and pleasure in their roles, which is a surefire indication they're doing what He meant them to do.

If God saw kingly potential in a small, lowly shepherd like our boy David, there's no reason to think He doesn't have some equally crucial purpose for each of us. Maybe we won't rule kingdoms, but we can each further the only kingdom that counts.

I gain peace and pleasure from writing, so I like to think that my novels serve His kingdom, and occasional reader feedback tells me how they do. He hasn't called me home yet, so I imagine He has more work for me, whether it's through writing or personal interaction or just being in the right place at the right time.

For people who have great suffering in their lives, the question is a tough one. Does their suffering serve some eternal purpose? I don't think any of us can fully grasp that idea. I do know that my own sister's suffering and her death at a young age directly led me to Christ. Who knows how many others followed that path because of her?

Maybe my purpose is found in a role the world finds mundane. Parenting can be thankless and edifying at the same time. Even if one's relationship with her child is strained, she may be the one model of Christ's unconditional love that child will ever know. A pretty heavy purpose, that.

Still more intriguing is the fact that I may have been chosen for one specific moment of service for the kingdom, one word or brief action that will lead a lost soul to Him. I once learned after the fact that something I said off-the-cuff caused another person to turn to Christ. In case I've been chosen for many such moments, it's my job to keep my mind and heart open to those opportunities. Because if *that* ain't purpose, I don't know what is. ⌁ Trish

TODAY'S PRAYER

Heavenly Father, thank You that You created each of us with a specific purpose in mind. Thank You that each of us has been hand-chosen for something important, whether that something is long-term service or a single moment in time.

Even if I never consciously recognize my purpose, Lord, please grace me with the ability to fulfill it according to Your will. Thank You for the honor of being a part of the kingdom.

I Just Got Comfortable

Yet the LORD longs to be gracious to you;
therefore he will rise up to show you compassion.

ISAIAH 30:18

The blogger asked, "What's the most romantic thing your husband did for you?"

Asked me to marry him at the foot of the cellar stairs? Volunteered to gut the fish we caught on our honeymoon? Bought me a luggage scale? (Apparently he was moved with compassion at the memory of me on my knees while curbside at the airport, jettisoning underwear and stuffing blue jeans in my purse to prevent an overage charge.)

There was that time he handed me the remote and said, "Watch whatever you want to watch."

"Really?"

"Yeah. I'm going out to the garage."

It was romantic when he washed my hair after a bulging disc flattened me. He draped a garbage bag over the end of the couch to which I was glued and puddled one end of the garbage bag in a five-gallon bucket. As I watched his strong, flannel-clad arms as he poured warm water over my hair, his kindness seemed so Jesus-like. So tender.

The *most* romantic moment of our life together?

When he brought me coffee on the balcony of our rental villa in Tuscany.

When he wrote my name in the raked gravel of a Japanese garden.

When he bought space on the JumboTron at a Packers game to tell the Monday Night Football viewing audience—pretty much everybody—that he loved me.

Oh, wait. Those things happened to someone else.

I did have a list of romantic gestures from which to choose to answer the blogger. Sweet moments when my husband's expressions of love made me say, "How romantic!"

Like the other day. He got out of his recliner.

We'd nestled into our quiet-evening-alone-together routine—he in his recliner and me in my chair that daily reminds me why I should have purchased a rocker. There's something "off" about that chair. Looks nice but sits funny, like a salad dressing with too much vinegar or stuffing with half a teaspoon too much sage.

I'd found the perfect angle, though. Throw pillows just so. Feet propped up on the ottoman. Book in hand. And my cup of tea?

In the microwave, two rooms away.

"Let me get it for you." My husband, the most romantic guy in the world at that moment, rose out of his chair. Left his own comfort. To serve me.

He rose to show me compassion. Just like Jesus does.

"Let Me get that for you," He says.

"I'm worried about my kids, Lord."

"Let Me get that for you."

"I can't think of a response to the woman at work who wants to drag me into her cauldron of gossip."

"Let Me get that for you."

"I'm having a hard time with _____ [fill in the blank]."

He rises to show me compassion and says, "Let Me get that for you."

He doesn't just resign Himself to be gracious or reluctantly agree to cut me some slack. He *longs* to be gracious to me. He's *looking* for ways to bless me. How divinely romantic! — Cynthia

TODAY'S PRAYER

Lord, every day You express Your love. I'm moved
that You move on my behalf, that comfort has never
meant more to You than my need.

What Are You Doing Here, Elijah?

Have no fear of sudden disaster or of the ruin
that overtakes the wicked, for the LORD will be at your side
and will keep your foot from being snared.
PROVERBS 3:25–26

In 1 Kings, Elijah called out to God to show Baal's followers who really ruled the roost, and the Lord answered his prayer with a very dramatic show. "Then the fire of the LORD fell," it says in chapter 18, verse 38, "and burned up the sacrifice, the wood, the stones and the soil, and also licked up the water in the trench." How cool was that? Don't we just love it when God's hand rests upon us for the world to see that we're *His*? He saves us from a bad situation and we're reminded that He's in charge, that He is able, that He is faithful.

It's worth noting here that, not long after God's fire display, Elijah drew the wrath of a vengeful woman named Jezebel. And what was the first thing he did? He ran for his life, first to Judah, then into the wilderness, and later into a mountain cave to hide out.

We're so much like Elijah, aren't we? Why can't we ever seem to remember that God's love and grace aren't given for just one situation, that He doesn't just answer one prayer and move on?

Many years ago, I found myself miserable in a day job that seemed to take everything out of me. At the end of the day, there never seemed to be enough creativity in me to put ten words on a page. My dreams of a writing career had begun to evaporate, and the stress of working a day job only added to the spiral. I'd built up my savings to where I had enough money to cover me for a year. I decided to take a chance on myself, and I quit my day job and settled into the writer life.

But that first book didn't sell, and before I knew it, I was out of time—and money. Deflated, I started my search for another day job. But finding another job proved to be next to impossible. The straits grew quite dire, and just about the time I ran out of options, a couple of miracles (including a job offer) snatched me back from the edge of losing everything.

Over the years, I've never forgotten that season. And recently, when my company was purchased by another one and my peers began talking of severance packages and job searches, it wasn't the last-minute save or God's promised grace and care that I remembered. It was the fear and anxiety of the decline.

When Elijah told the story of God's arrival outside of the cave, he spoke of an earthquake, heavy winds, and fire. But God wasn't in any of those things. No, instead, God was found in the soft, gentle whisper.

And so as I wait for the future to unfold, that's what I hang onto. I remind myself that God sustains throughout the trials, and His answer always comes. Even if it does come at the last possible moment.

~ Sandie

TODAY'S PRAYER

· · · · · · · · · · · · · · · · · · ·

Lord God, thank You for the promise that,
after the earthquake and the driving rain,
You will come to us in a sweet and gentle way.

There's Always Room
for Cheesecake

Rejoice always, pray continually.
1 THESSALONIANS 5:16-17

In the face of TV and newspaper reports of famines, floods, fires, earthquakes, tsunamis, and tornadoes, it's easy to understand the "pray continually" element of this Bible verse. Stories of war, foreclosures, and crime, though, make the "rejoice always" part not so easy. After all, according to Webster, the very word *rejoice* means "celebrate, exult, be glad." So how's a believer to feel joy when confronted with all the horrible things going on in our world?

A very similar discussion took place just last week while dining with friends when, for every negative item our friend, Pete, quoted from the evening news, Dan offered a positive:

Pete: "Gas prices are up. Again!"

Dan: "Did you hear about the kids who set up a car wash at the gas station and then donated the money to help a family displaced by a house fire?"

Pete: "That crazy governor of ours is talking about raising taxes. *Again!*"

Dan: "And did you hear that he launched a program to protect nursing-home residents from neglect and abuse?"

On and on it continued, through the soup-and-salad course, as the bowl of braised potatoes went back and forth, all but drowning out my carefully selected dinner music and dragging our formerly upbeat moods down, down, down, like the waxy white drips on the centerpiece candles.

While my guests halfheartedly sipped decaf coffee and poked at the very-berry cheesecake I'd spent hours baking and decorating, I turned off the stereo and grabbed my guitar. They pretty much ignored my strumming. Pretty much ignored those first few songs too. But when I launched into the old standby, "How Great Thou Art," they joined in crooning lyrics committed to heart as children. Back then we might have been old enough to memorize the *words*, but we were a long, long way from the maturity and wisdom required to grasp the true meaning behind stanzas that spoke of the awesome wonder found in every forest glade and birdsong, from every mountain and babbling brook, and, yes, even in the rolling thunder: *"He is there."*

For a while there, Pessimist Pete sang solo, tears shimmering in his eyes as the rhythmical praise of composer Carl Boberg passed his lips. "That on the cross, my burden gladly bearing, He bled and died to take away my sin."

Once the amen was sung, he sat back, a serene smile lighting his formerly gloomy face. "Well," he said, breaking the companionable silence, *"there's* a clear reminder that there has always been suffering and strife in this ol' world"—he took a sip of his decaf—"and that Jesus, by His supreme sacrifice, erased any excuse we frail humans can think up to rationalize our fears."

While we nodded our agreement, Pete requested a second helping of cheesecake. "And this time," he said, laughing, "I'm gonna enjoy every delectable calorie!" Loree

TODAY'S PRAYER

O Jesus, knowing that You loved me enough to suffer and die for my sins weakens my knees and fills my heart with gratefulness. Keep me always aware that, no matter how dire and dangerous this world might at times seems, You are there, strong and steadfast, extending Your promise of salvation to ease my fears. Amen and hallelujah!

Hey! Watch Where You're Going!

Direct my footsteps according to your word;
let no sin rule over me.

PSALM 119:133

One of my favorite ways of exercising is to walk on my treadmill. The logistics in my home dictate its placement. I can't have it facing a window, so I'm not able to pretend I'm walking outdoors like a normal person. Neither am I able to have face it toward the TV (unless I get rid of my couch, which could be a problem when friends come to visit—there's something less than cozy about sipping a cup of tea while sitting on a treadmill). I seldom listen to music while I walk, but I usually read for a mile or two.

And now I've confessed how *slowly* I walk on said treadmill. Others could never hold a book steady while exercising. I probably *could* sip tea during my activity. Hey, don't judge me. It's better than nothing, right?

One of the best things about reading novels while "working out" is that I get distracted by someone else's story, and before I know it, I've done the entire walk without once wishing it would hurry up and be over.

Sometimes, though, the distraction is too intense. More than once, I've learned a mini-lesson in Newton's laws of motion, when my forward-moving self has accidentally stepped just slightly off the moving track and met with rigid resistance. All kinds of acrobatics take place before I finally go down. One time this happened when I had a rocking chair a little too close to the back of the treadmill, so

I was unable to actually shoot off the conveyor belt. The chair kept me momentarily trapped there, bouncing around like a big bag of volleyballs, before I managed to roll myself off.

These are the moments when one is relieved to be alone and off camera.

It's so easy to get distracted from the path the Lord establishes for each one of us. Sometimes I focus too intently on what someone else is doing or has accomplished, and I fall out of step with what's important on *my* walk. So, too, many have taken just a few steps here, a few steps there, in directions they know can't possibly be meant for them—into a bar, when they know alcohol is a weakness; into an environment fraught with sexual temptation; into a conversation virtually guaranteed to lead to gossip; into a financial endeavor that hasn't for a moment been prayed over.

The writer of today's verse clearly knew the power of sin and how easily it can pull any one of us away from the blessings God has set out for our future. Occasionally, sin is like a dramatic fall from a cliff. Or a fast-moving treadmill. But more often than not, sin redirects our path one subtle step at a time. Before we know it, we're bouncing around like a big old bag of volleyballs, getting bruised, battered, and trying to crawl away from the consequences of our missteps. Divine guidance never looked so good! ⮕ Trish

TODAY'S PRAYER

Gracious Father, Your path is the one I want to follow every day and for the rest of my life. Please help me remember to seek Your guidance each morning and in all my decisions.

Snow Wonder

Like a snow-cooled drink at harvest time is a trustworthy messenger
to the one who sends him; he refreshes the spirit of his master.

PROVERBS 25:13

It's snowing as I write this. What month is it? Doesn't really matter. Here in northern Wisconsin, you could flip a calendar to any month of the year and it's likely there's been snow on that date somewhere in history. With the possible exception of July.

Our furnace has been called into action many times when it thought it was on summer vacation. The conversation it conducts with the air-conditioning unit goes something like this:

"Tag. You're it."

"I thought you had it."

"That was yesterday. Your turn."

The first snowfall in a season fascinates and intrigues, as if we conveniently don't remember the batch that finally melted a few months previously.

"Look! It's snowing!"

We rush to the windows of our offices and family rooms, mesmerized by the glitter falling from the sky.

Glitter loses some of its luster toward the end of winter. A sigh follows the words, "It's snowing again." Where the sound of the snow-plow once comforted—a reassuring reminder that the county guys care about our personal safety—when winter should have quit long ago, it grates like fingernails on asphalt.

But, oh, that first snowfall! Rain's fluffy but surprisingly-light-on-her-feet cousin. Angora shawls for the pine trees. An unstitched quilt for the tired lawn. A drink of once tepid air now chilled by shaved ice.

Kids and husbands beg to go out into the white. They ask for the privilege of shoveling or firing up the snowblower.

Yeah.

Those first flakes of snow make me dance, too, but not because I'm enamored with a snowblower. They signal the end of canning season. Hallelujah.

Some years, the tomato crop doesn't know enough to come in out of the…snow. Though the vines had sense enough to shrivel on schedule, the tomatoes continue to ripen, spotting the garden plot more thoroughly than acne the day before the prom.

Frugal enough not to waste a harvest, I'll haul in the produce with a bushel basket again, take it into the house again, dip the orbs in boiling water to remove the skins again, stuff the tomatoes into jars again, fit the jars with flats and rings again, process the jars in a hot-water bath again, cool the jars again, label them again…

"It's snowing!"

What a relief. The snow means I can put a lid on any false guilt and declare I'm done canning for another year. Grateful for the harvest and for the ability to make chili or venison stew midwinter, I'm also blessed when the snow signals the end of canning season.

Snow at the end of harvest—sweet relief.

Am I? Am I a relief for others?

When I show up on the scene, do I refresh others like an invigorating, relief-bringing first snowfall? What would have to change in my understanding and application of God's grace for that to happen?

— Cynthia

TODAY'S PRAYER

· ·

God of Creation, keeper of the storehouses of snow,
keep me so sensitive to the needs of others and to the
messages You have for me to deliver that my faithfulness
to bear Your hope will refresh others and refresh You.

Can't Get No Satisfaction

Surely, LORD, you bless the righteous;
you surround them with your favor as with a shield.

PSALM 5:12

I had a laundry list of things I wanted when I finally purchased my first home. It had to have a fenced backyard with lots of green grass for Sophie to roll around in; I needed a third bedroom for an office, a second bathroom so I never had to share, a connected garage and laundry room, and a lot of light filtering through a ton of windows. Oh, and I wanted my mortgage payment to stay within two hundred dollars of the monthly rent I already paid.

"Enough already," a good friend cautioned me. "You can't have everything, Sandie. You'll learn soon enough that you're going to have to compromise."

But why?

I'd waited a very long time to purchase my first home all on my own. I had prayed and hoped and dreamed; I'd cut out pictures from magazines and catalogs and glued them into a "dream book." I priced a new sofa for the home I hadn't yet purchased, and I chose paint colors for the master bedroom and the office I hadn't even seen.

For some reason, God created me with the ability to see things from a hopeful perspective. People have often remarked about what a "big dreamer" I am. "Sandie's not easily satisfied," an ex-boyfriend once declared to one of my closest friends. "I just don't think anyone can ever live up to her expectations."

I wasn't particularly sad about the fact that we broke up soon after that, but I do sometimes wish I'd had the opportunity to tell him he'd never have had to live up to my hopes and dreams for my life because they didn't really have anything to do with him. Instead, they had everything to do with God.

"I guess I'm just a 'glass half empty' kind of guy," he'd told me early on, in a tone that let me know I'd been warned. "I just don't believe in getting my hopes too high; I expect the worst and hope for the best, and that way I'm almost never disappointed."

I remember thinking, *Wow. What a sad way to live!* I suppose I'm the exact opposite of him. I like to expect the best and hope it won't be the worst, and my glass is mostly full. I tend to revel in the grace and favor promised to me in the Scriptures, and I often make plans based on that favor. I mean, I'm not saying I've never been deflated or had my hopes dashed, but when I read that God's favor surrounds me like a shield, I consciously wear that shield out into the world. Sometimes it gets knocked around a bit, and in a few cases it's let me down, but I still don't leave home without it! Does that mean I'm never satisfied, or does it mean that I just know how big my God is? — Sandie

TODAY'S PRAYER

. . . .

Father God, let the challenges of this day be seasoned
with the realization that your favor surrounds me like a shield.
I've done nothing to earn it, and I don't have to ask for it
or figure it out, which makes the gift all the more sweet!

"Hoover" You Waiting For?

*For the eyes of the Lord range throughout the earth
to strengthen those whose hearts are fully committed to him.*

2 CHRONICLES 16:9

This morning, in the middle of a cleaning frenzy, the telephone rang. I really, *really* hate it when that happens, especially when Hoover and I are workin' some serious moves to Hall & Oates' "Private Eyes." In my rush to quiet the incessant ringing, I tripped over Hoover's cord and nearly landed face-first in a pile of Pledge-soaked rags. "Go soak your head in a bucket of Pine-Sol!" is what I wanted to bark into the receiver. Fortunately for my friend, who'd called in search of a sympathetic shoulder, I merely growled, "Hello?"

Turns out Tina's daughter—long embroiled in a turbulent relationship—almost left her husband.

It was the "almost" that had upset Tina. "I hate to see any marriage end," she cried, "but I can't stand knowing that my bipolar son-in-law, Joseph, could snap and turn the kids into domestic violence statistics." On the heels of a shaky sigh, she added, "Where is *God* in all of this?"

My heart ached for her. As a mom and grandmom myself, I identified with her fear and helplessness.

I took a breath and summoned divine guidance, because this sure didn't seem like the right time to say "Look to Jesus in your time of need" or "God is your refuge and your strength." As she recited Joseph's non-Christian flaws, I was reminded of the biblical king Asa and his battle with Israel's Baasha. Instead of turning to God for help, Asa purchased protection by way of a treaty with yet another king…and it cost him. Big-time.

Tina was listing Joseph-the-unbeliever's latest wrongdoings when the story of pianist Andor Földes came to my mind. He was barely sixteen and embroiled in the most tumultuous year of his life when Franz Liszt's last surviving student asked him to play. Though it was the last thing he felt like doing, Földes chose the most difficult sonatas in his repertoire—Schumann, Bach, Beethoven—and when he finished, renowned Emil von Sauer kissed his forehead. "After *my* first lesson with Liszt," said von Sauer, "he kissed my forehead. 'Take good care of that kiss,' he said, 'for it is from Beethoven himself.' I have been waiting for years to find a student worthy to pass it on to." Quite a hefty responsibility, one I'm sure young Földes, like his talented predecessors, took quite seriously when it was his turn to hand down the esteemed tradition.

By contrast, God's grace requires nothing of us but belief in Him and acceptance of the generous gift of his love. I'll keep right on praying for Tina, for her daughter and her grandchildren, and for Joe, too, that he might one day bask in the joy that goes hand in hand with knowing the amazing comfort of God's grace. — Loree

TODAY'S PRAYER

O Father divine, keep me aware that, simply by walking in
grace, I can embrace faith and all glorious wonder that comes
with it. Remind me, Lord, to set aside time each day
to reflect and meditate upon the divine providence
of You in my life, so that I never forget
what an amazing comfort is Your love!

Still Waiting!

The Lord is not slow in keeping his promise, as some understand slowness.
Instead he is patient with you, not wanting anyone to perish,
but everyone to come to repentance.

2 PETER 3:9

I remember the day my son-in-law got baptized in church, broke into a huge grin, and publicly proclaimed, "Jesus is Lord." Of course, I cried; as much as I loved him, I had worried because he never seemed all that interested in knowing about Christ and what He offered. Hearing him happily give his life to the Lord was a dream come true.

And then my next thought was, "Okay, Lord, I'm ready now. All my kids are saved. Come on back!"

That was about a decade ago. I think we all know how that plan worked out. But I do catch myself thinking like the person who frantically runs to catch a bus before it's actually time for departure and then gets impatient about how long it's taking to get going. *I'm on it now, so let's get going already!* Or I think that way about my loved ones. Once me and mine are onboard, isn't it time to go?

Uh, no, apparently not.

I'm thrilled to have come to Christ before He comes back for us, aren't you? We see in today's verse that the Lord wants everyone to wise up and come to repentance. Of course, history has shown that that isn't going to happen, thanks to a little thing we call free will. And God knows full well who is and isn't going to make that decision within the lifetime allotted here on earth.

I find it fascinating to think about that one last person yet to make the decision, prompting Christ's return. I sometimes picture the occurrence like a hugely amplified one-millionth-customer celebration, where that one person walks through the turnstile and sets off a marching band, cheerleaders jumping all over the place, and confetti raining down everywhere. Sometimes I wonder if that person has been born yet. Wouldn't it be a blast to play a role in that last person's coming to Christ?

Which brings us to some interesting wording in today's verse. "He is patient with you." Certainly the Lord is patient with His children as He waits for us to accept His free gift of salvation. But might He also be showing patience with us with regard to our efforts at sharing Him with others? Our efforts at demonstrating His grace by our actions?

I think so. Just a few verses farther down, Peter says, "You ought to live holy and godly lives as you look forward to the day of God and speed its coming."

Speed His coming? Well, all right! I thoroughly love my life here on earth, but I'm so eager to meet Him in person! And I want everyone I know to meet Him too. ⸙ Trish

TODAY'S PRAYER
· · · · · · · · · · · · · · · · · · · ·

Gracious Lord, You know the specific number of souls who
will eventually join You in the clouds, and I look forward to that
glorious day. If there is a word or action I should be sharing
to hasten Your return, I ask that You put the word on my lips
and the action in my step. Thank You for the privilege
of playing a role in Your ultimate plan.

The View from Here

The LORD upholds all those who fall and lifts up all who are bowed down.
PSALM 145:14

What a view!"

It's a phrase that pulses through the dialogue between prospective home owners and their bright-eyed, smooth-talking realty agents.

"So, are you ready to make an offer?" an agent asks, with cell phone in one hand and pen in the other.

"The kitchen's outdated. The bathrooms need upgrades. The bedrooms are cramped, and there's one too few of them for our family's needs. "

"But will you look at that view!"

"Sold."

It may not happen that simply, but a great view is often on the list of must-haves for home buyers. When I dream about the ideal home, the first frame in my mental slide show isn't the slick countertops or the walk-in closets or the jetted tub. It's the view. A wide expanse of water, a smooth stretch of sand, mountains, woodlands, a manicured lawn, and an Eden-like garden. Yes, I know a real-estate agent would have a rough time matching a property to my wish list...and an even harder time reconciling it to our family budget. That's why it's a dream rather than a plan. My dream has a view.

As longevity and arthritis curled her spine like a shepherd's hook, an elderly woman from my home church found her view reduced to the patch of carpet, the sidewalk, the floor tiles right in front of her feet. She leaned heavily on a cane, which I first assumed was because of her bad hip. But I now wonder if it wasn't to keep her from tipping over onto her forehead.

Cowlick to bunion, she probably rounded up to five feet on her driver's license when she could still see over the steering wheel. Those of us who cared about her learned to bend down and look up in order to carry on a conversation with the bent woman.

I can't imagine having such a restricted view of life—carpet fibers and thresholds. The scuffed toes of people's shoes. Crawling things and cracks in the asphalt.

Wouldn't you think her spirit would be bowed down too?

Far from it. Though her physical gaze was fixed on the ground beneath her, her spiritual gaze was locked on Jesus. Her attitude wasn't grounded; it soared.

Unable to make eye contact with people, she maintained constant eye contact with the Lord. No wonder her life remained one of irrepressible joy.

That's the secret, isn't it? It's all about the view. When I focus on the potholes at my feet, the toenail fungus and muddy footprints of life, I live bent. But even when circumstances force my attention downward, I have viewpoint options. Despite concerns that threaten to curl my spine, I can have a clear, unrestricted line of sight to the Author of grace. When my heart locks gazes with Him, He straightens my internal posture and changes my outlook so I see life from His perspective.

Will you look at that amazing view! ⟶ Cynthia

TODAY'S PRAYER
. . . .

Lord God, impress upon my heart the incredible privilege
of catching Your eye, the incomparable joy waiting
for me when I stop focusing on the junk at my feet
and look up instead. Thank You for the breathtaking,
unrestricted view of Your grace.

Badge of Dishonor

Bear with each other and forgive one another if any of you has a grievance against someone. Forgive as the Lord forgave you.
COLOSSIANS 3:13

Elaine had endured a tumultuous adolescence that left her with battle scars she made no effort to cover up. She was very young when her mother had been killed by a drunk driver—and she'd once been held up at gunpoint, which ingrained another dramatic experience for her. It didn't take long in our acquaintance for me to recognize the drunk driver and the gunman as badges pinned to her identity, and she frequently vowed to never forgive either of them. "My anger toward them is part of who I am. I'll never let it go."

Really? I found that so sad. I often spoke about the concept of the supernatural forgiveness I'd found through my faith, and I made promises to Elaine about the joy she could experience if she made a conscious choice to forgive those two strangers who'd played pivotal (albeit devastating) roles in her life. I sent her Scripture verses and chatted with her for hours on end, but it always came down to the same refusal to let go. Not only had these two men become an integral part of her, but they also provided a flag that she could plant on any hilltop at any time as an excuse for bad behavior. It became clear that she had no intention of ever setting aside those flags, and the more I tried to reason with her, the more her anger turned on me along with those men. Finally, one day when I found myself holding my own bitterness and unforgiveness—toward Elaine—I took it to the throne, found myself washed clean of it, and turned and walked away. The only times I've ever looked back have been those times when I've prayed for my former friend, which I've done a lot over the years.

There have been seasons in my life where I've displayed my own flags of unforgiving bitterness, so I understood Elaine's penchant for hanging on to them. But one thing I've learned from my journey with Jesus is that a tremendous sacrifice was made so that I might be forgiven, so that I might be pure and clean enough to sit at the feet of a Father who adores me. How could I possibly hold on to anger, bitterness, and resentment while peering into the crystal-clear eyes of that loving Father?

The great philosopher and anti-apartheid activist Nelson Mandela once said, "Resentment is like drinking poison and waiting for it to kill your enemy." Truer words outside of Scripture have never been spoken. Is there someone you haven't forgiven? Has that bitterness been around so long that it's become a part of your identity? Make a choice today. Replace it with a badge of humility, and become a reflection of the unending grace extended to you. — Sandie

TODAY'S PRAYER

For every offense I've ever held on to, for every time
I've refused to grant forgiveness and then sought some
for myself, I ask that You cleanse me in Your shed
and living blood, Lord Jesus. Help me to reflect Your love,
this day and every day.

A Stinky Situation

The LORD is good to all; he has compassion on all he has made.

PSALM 145:9

Baltimore is under attack!

The assailants? Pentatomidae, the largest family of insects in the superfamily Pentatomoidea of the Hemiptera order.

In plain English, we've been invaded by stinkbugs.

Protected by a hideous shell, these nightmare-inducing creepy-crawlies don't bite (like mosquitoes) or sting (like wasps)...though they *could,* if they had a mind to poke their proboscises into human flesh. Fortunately, they're too busy devouring apples and peaches in the neighboring orchards or feasting on the Beefeater tomatoes in my garden.

Just knowing that they were outside and multiplying by the millions (literally!) was bad enough. But then the disgusting li'l critters rode indoors on our shoulders and got to work at draining the green from my houseplants!

Like creatures from a science-fiction movie, they made their way from Asia to Baltimore by way of Pittsburgh. (So I think it's only fair that Steel Town citizens send their "Terrible Towels" to Charm City; as we use them to render stinkbugs unconscious, we might also diminish the rivalry that exists between Ravens and Steelers fans.)

During those first weeks of the buggy assault, I read every stinkbug article I could get my hands on. Spiders can't eat them (the shells are too hard), and the gag-a-maggot odor protects them from birds. Unlike worms, they don't enrich the earth; unlike bees, they can't pollinate plants. Despite years of tedious experiments, scientists haven't found anything that will kill the arrogant pests that have an uncanny ability to stand on two hind legs, waving pronged forefeet as if to say, "We're stayin', and there ain't a thing you can do about it. Neener, neener!"

One day, I spied a stinkbug on the kitchen floor, unafraid and in no particular hurry to reach its destination. But then, why would it feel rushed or frightened when God blessed it with a hardy constitution and no known enemies?

To that point, I'd called them ugly. Unsettling. Useless. But as I watched it waddle toward the dining room, I got an inkling of what the Almighty might have had in mind when He fashioned the little tomato demolishers.

"The LORD is good to all," says Psalm 145:9, "and he has compassion on all he has made." *Perhaps,* I thought, gently gathering the little bug into a nest of facial tissue, *God put stinkbugs on the earth not to pollinate flowers or mulch soil, not even to terrorize humans...but to remind us that if He could love and protect stinkbugs, of all things, how much more must He want to love and care for us...the beings He made in His own image and likeness!*

Like the stinkbug, I moved toward the powder room, unafraid and in no particular hurry. "You're going into the sewer," I said, "and there isn't a thing you can do about it. Neener, neener!" ⏤ Loree

TODAY'S PRAYER
. . . .

Father, my Father, Your power lives in the vastness of the sky
and the depths of the oceans. No being ever formed
of Your hands deserves Your all-inclusive, protective love,
yet there it is for the taking, even for the smallest
(and stinkiest) of Your creations. Let me see
each of these through Your eyes.

At Least Something in Common

All the believers were together and had everything in common.

ACTS 2:44

I'm a selfish gal. I'm not proud of the fact, but I recognize it. I'm so bad that, when I had a houseful of people living with me, I had a secret chocolate drawer near my computer. I kept chocolate out in the open for others too—but I hoarded my special stash in case the general supply ran out.

You may wonder what selfishness has to do with today's verse. At first glance, the verse sounds as if it refers to the joy of gathering with like-minded Christians. And that's what we all seek when we choose the church we'll attend on Sundays, right? We want to be sure the pastor's teaching fits with our perception of God's Word or makes a mighty strong argument for why our perception needs tweaking. If we find that, won't the congregation of believers eventually have "everything in common"?

Yet within the context of the rest of the chapter, the verse is actually about sharing our wealth with others. The next verse talks about believers "selling their property and possessions" and giving "to anyone as he had need." I've even read a commentary that says this was the basic idea old Karl Marx was shooting for—but his followers enforced the concept through violence and imprisonment. I can imagine how much time in the gulag I'd be saddled with if they got a load of my chocolate drawer.

Now, I'm not *heartless*. Like most people, when I stop and consider those truly less fortunate than me, my heart opens wider. An ad airs about the International Fellowship of Christians and Jews and I give with little hesitation. I see an adorable, impoverished Honduran child via World Vision and gladly sign up as his monthly sponsor. I walk down a city street, see the growing number of homeless people, and start passing out dollar bills I would have easily spent on chocolate, lattes, or any other number of frivolous indulgences.

I need to do that more often. I give at church, just like your typical attendee. That's easy enough—I write out a check as part of my church preparation, just like putting on mascara and making sure my Bible is in the car. Certainly that kind of giving is enough. We're only instructed to tithe, after all. Most churches delegate a good portion of congregants' donations to charitable causes, so it's not as if our tithes are only used for administrating the church's business.

Still, there's something about hands-on giving that brings out the real warm fuzzies *and* keeps me appreciative of how blessed my own circumstances are. I admit, I won't sell *all* my possessions and goods in order to give to everyone as he has need. I'm simply not that generous, I'm afraid. But if I refrain from buying a possession here or a designer coffee there, I can more readily give according to my neighbor's needs in a way that will bless us both. — Trish

TODAY'S PRAYER

Heavenly Father, Your blessings on my life are without
question. I ask that You draw my eyes and my heart
to specific needs I can address in my fellow human beings.
Thank You for the joy such giving brings.

Ears to Hear

How gracious he will be when you cry for help!
As soon as he hears, he will answer you.

ISAIAH 30:19

A ten-year-old boy with intense ear pain needs immediate attention. Every mom knows that. The clinic was closed for the night,
so we took our son to the emergency room for what turned into hours
of waiting and a "we'll never forget this" memory.

Not one to complain (he still isn't), Matt had apparently endured
the pain in his right ear for quite a while before he told me about it. No
doubt Matt had an ear infection, one that couldn't wait until morning,
judging by the distress on our son's face.

The emergency-room doctor checked Matt's medical records,
examined Matt's left ear, then examined his right, and said, "I see he's
had tubes inserted."

"No, that's our other son. Luke's the one with all the ear infections.
Matt hasn't had much trouble since he had his tonsils out at four."
Which, I wanted to add, *should be right there on his medical records.*

The doctor pulled away from peering into Matt's ear to look at
me. "Well, he has a tube in this ear. The left one must have fallen out."

I would have remembered if Matt had had ear-drainage tubes
inserted. I distinctly remembered the procedure with his younger
brother. No mama easily takes to the idea of her child going under
anesthesia...or forgets how hard it can be on the child when he
comes out of it. Luke screamed in the recovery room. He wasn't a
happy boy after that procedure. This much I knew. Luke had ear
tubes. Matt did not.

"It's green. Right there," Doctor Well-oh-yeah said, gesturing with some kind of needle-nosed instrument he aimed at Matt's ear canal.

A minute later, we all stared at the tiny green tube the doctor had extracted from my son's ear and laid on the stainless-steel tray.

Using two sets of needle-nosed something or others, the doctor poked at a loose edge on the tube. It uncurled.

A gum wrapper.

How did a gum wrapper get rolled that tightly? How did it get embedded into Matt's eardrum? The obvious answers involved a ten-year-old boy, one who shrugged his shoulders and said, "I dunno."

One would think he could hear better with a gum wrapper removed from his ear. I don't remember noticing an improvement. He was still a ten-year-old boy.

As embarrassing as it was for all of us to chalk up an ER visit to a stick of Doublemint, it made a memory. As I thought about that incident today, it made me all the more appreciative of a God who hears. Clearly. No encumbrance. Nothing in the way. Nothing to distract Him from loving us and wanting to bless us.

I appreciate a God whose mighty hand hovers over the SEND button, eager to set answers in motion the moment He hears our cry for help. Our God hears everything. And in yet one more expression of His grace, He acts as soon as He hears. Sometimes sooner.
⟶ Cynthia

TODAY'S PRAYER

Father God, I worship You. Great listening, caring,
attentive Lord, thank You for the answers I haven't seen yet
but can know they are on their way because that's who You are.

Crisis Intervention

The LORD has heard my cry for mercy; the LORD accepts my prayer.
PSALM 6:9

Divorce used to be a topic that good Christians didn't talk about or even sometimes admit to. However, on the landscape of today's America, divorce is everywhere. And so are the hurting people who have survived it.

I hadn't yet turned my life over to God when I impulsively married the wrong man, so I didn't quite know where to turn when the relationship became abusive. Alcohol, violence, name-calling, threats, and bullying became a regular part of my life. At its best, my marriage seemed more like two children playing house; at its worst, I became isolated hundreds of miles from my family and friends. I allowed a lifelong battle with my weight and a dysfunctional relationship with food to overwhelm me; I became fearful, unhealthy, even severely agoraphobic. When one of my husband's coworkers, someone I hardly knew, suggested that I stage an intervention about his abuse of alcohol (and his wife), I remember thinking, "An intervention for him? I'm the one who needs an intervention!"

My conversation with that virtual stranger proved to be a life-changing event for me. As my alcoholic husband drifted off into a drunken coma that Saturday night, I sat on the sofa in the dark, praying to a God I wasn't even sure was there.

My husband had found my spiral notebooks of story ideas and destroyed them, along with precious mementos of my past and the addresses and phone numbers of anyone to whom I might have reached out for help. "What happened to that girl I used to be?" I asked the ceiling, realizing only much later that this was the form prayer had taken. "Remember her? I knew how to love and be loved; I had dreams of writing big Hollywood movies and living near the beach." It was at that moment that I realized how accurate I'd been in assessing my need for a drastic and immediate intervention, and I vowed to the ceiling to perform *my own*! Intervention, that is.

Three months later, I had mastered many of my fears, at least enough to function outside the door of our apartment. Soon I packed my little car with only what it would hold and escaped to Los Angeles, where I eventually went to film school and learned to write screenplays. I couldn't afford to live at the beach, but I certainly did visit often. Still carrying those visions of the girl I once was and the woman I one day hoped to be in my back pocket as a reminder, I one day met the Savior who had designed them (and me). He made it very clear that He had heard my prayers and answered them, and He miraculously extended something to me I didn't quite understand—but I jumped at it! He offered me the grace to move forward. ~ Sandie

TODAY'S PRAYER

· · · · · · · · · · · · · · · · · · ·

Thank You, Lord Jesus, for Your magnificent hearing—
the hearing that listened when I cried—and Your stellar vision—
the vision that saw into my future and showed it to me
in quick and quiet glimpses when I needed them
so desperately. Help me to continue the journey
toward that woman I hope to be.

Come Blow Your Horn

*Let someone else praise you, and not your own mouth;
an outsider, and not your own lips.*

PROVERBS 27:2

I wasn't one of those kids who performed with the high-school orchestra, and I didn't join the marching band either. Mostly that's because the only instrument available was the trumpet, and even back then, I wasn't any good at tooting my own horn.

Oh, I have no trouble at all boasting about my husband, my kids, and my grandkids. They're as perfect as feet-on-the-ground humans can be. They're gorgeous. And smart. Successful, loving, and kind. They're linked directly to me, either by marriage or by blood, and because of that, I automatically get bragging rights. (Just ask anyone whose bangs have been mussed as I whip out the accordion-like photo holder in my wallet!) But praising the attributes and accomplishments of people I love isn't the same as singing my *own* praises. Not by a long shot!

I'm the first to admit that patting myself on the back is physically impossible (what if I dislocate a shoulder?) and emotionally uncomfortable. A dangerous thing to admit, considering what I do for a living. In the days of Hemingway, publishers could afford to promote authors and their books. These days, PR and marketing is a do-it-yourself—or a do-it-or-die—proposition. I have a fear of heights, so walking the tightrope as I try to find a healthy balance of what to say about myself and what to leave out, is downright nerve-racking.

Family, friends, even fellow authors cite the "Don't hide your light under a bushel" verse to coax me out into the open. So why does this former sang-for-my-supper entertainer have such a hard time standing in the limelight, when my gifts are God-given and, for the most part, used to glorify Him? (As soon as I find the answer to that one, you'll be the first to know.)

In the meantime, I thank the good Lord for blessing me with readers—men, women, and kids—who write to tell me what they did (and sometimes, what they didn't!) like about my stories. Their words confirm my decision to write faith-based fiction rather than "the other stuff." I'm honored that, of all the books they could choose, they so often choose mine. I'm proud that, over the years, so many readers have become treasured friends.

I'm reminded of the rhyme my gal pals and I recited while skipping rope on the playground: "First comes love, then comes marriage…"

In this case, first came grace, then came faith, and I can no more take credit for my so-called talents or gifts than I could play "Lady of Spain" on that bugle without making the audience cringe and cover their ears. What I am and what I accomplish in this life is solely by the grace of God.

And that's the triumph I'm happy to trumpet about! — Loree

TODAY'S PRAYER

O Lord, I stand before You humbled by the generosity
of Your love. That You would choose me as a child of God
fills me with awe and joy, and it will be by Your grace that
I live a life that echoes that confidence and love.
Praise to Your holy name, now and forever!

A Reason to Sing

The LORD has chastened me severely,
but he has not given me over to death.

When I consider how my life has played out so far, I'm amazed at how little hardship I've suffered. I mean, I've experienced plenty of loss, heartbreak, and problems in the financial and health areas, but relative to many of my friends and acquaintances? A cakewalk. Maybe it's because the Lord knows what a powder puff I am; I don't know.

And I always hesitate to look at anything adverse that's happening in my life or anyone else's as the Lord's "chastening," as the term is used in today's verse. One only has to read Job to figure out that we can't ever expect to understand why bad things happen to good people, other than those consequences obviously tied to bad decisions we've made—and I've experienced a few of *those* chastenings.

Still, I do find myself trying to ferret out why certain bad things have come my way—the bad things that don't seem to be the result of stupid or sinful choices on my part. Are they just part of living in a sinful world, or is the Lord trying to tell me something? If I'm going through a bad time because He wants me to figure something out, I want to figure it out toot sweet.

I can't say I've been highly successful in that.

It's interesting to note that Psalm 118 and the few psalms before it are always read (sung, actually) at Passover. It makes sense that the Jews would celebrate deliverance from death when commemorating the original Passover, right? And Psalm 118 contains a few other nuggets of joy, including, "Give thanks to the LORD, for he is good; his love endures forever" (verses 1, 29). Wonderful stuff that sets off familiar worship songs in my mind.

But consider it a step further. If verses like these are typically sung during the Passover meal, chances are good that they were sung at the Last Supper. Matthew even tells us that, after Jesus broke the bread and drank the wine and proclaimed the sacrifice He was about to make for all mankind, "they" sang (Matthew 26:30).

Do you think He sang too? Do you think He sang the Passover psalms? Can you imagine Him singing about how wonderful the day was, how there was reason for rejoicing, how God's love endures forever, right before He was to be taken to the cross? And can you imagine His rejoicing that God had not given Him over to death?

Kind of puts a *real* eternal perspective on things, doesn't it? If Jesus wasn't being given over to death, certainly none of us are, if we've given our hearts to Him.

Kind of makes me want to sing. ⌐ Trish

TODAY'S PRAYER

Heavenly Lord Jesus, I praise You for the sacrifice You made
for me, and I treasure the fact that You maintained Your joy
in God even as You faced a painful earthly death. I ask that
You help me to keep my focus eternal, especially
when hardship or suffering touches my life.
Thank You that, no matter what,
I will never truly be given over to death.

Strength Training

LORD, be gracious to us; we long for you.
Be our strength every morning, our salvation in time of distress.

ISAIAH 33:2

I wonder if the Lord chuckles at us like we do when watching a toddler boy take a professional bodybuilder stance, flexing his muscles and growling, as if that makes him stronger.

Two sons and three grandsons into this adventure of life, I've watched at least five versions of "Show me how strong you are." The two-foot-nothing child would push up his shirtsleeves to his shoulders, make tiny fists with his tiny hands, lean forward as he fluffs his biceps and forearms, and shake with the extreme effort. Grrrrrr!

How could we do anything but laugh? Thirty pounds of mini muscles pretending to be strong. A ball of fury run on a single AAA battery.

And…that's me. Not the thirty pounds part, unless you use one of those "to the sixth power" symbols. But I act like a delusional toddler when I think I'm strong enough to endure difficulty without Him, strong enough to resist temptation without Him, strong enough to get myself out of trouble—*thank You very much*—without Him. Like a toddler growling at an invisible foe. How cute!

And how utterly hysterical that picture must seem to Almighty God. "Aren't those humans adorable when they flex their muscles?"

"See how strong I am" is a statement that often immediately precedes a nasty fall. "Watch me juggle these forty things" foretells that something's about to drop. "Look how far I can jump" comes right before "Ow! Call 911!"

And still the Lord stands poised to give all of Himself for all of my need, despite my delusions of strength, my miscalculations about the difference between the size of my muscles and the scope of the giants I face.

One would think that someone like me, who thrives on efficiency and organizes her errands so every parking lot is a right-hand turn, would have learned the lesson long ago. My strength is puny in light of His. So what does He do? He offers to loan me His—the unfailing, bigger-than-any-problem, never-runs-out-of-batteries, perpetual, instant, overcoming Conqueror kind of strength. He says, "Ask Me. I'll be your strength."

Help me out here, Lord.

"Done."

Well, let me have a chance to tell you why it is I need a little more strength.

"A *little* more?"

Okay, a lot more.

"Doesn't matter the reason. You need it. You'll have it."

What an incredible gift!

I'm asked to handle a difficult task. Oh, you too? Sounds doable until I get a few minutes into it and realize it's far beyond my natural abilities. I'm unqualified. Unprepared. Not knowledgeable enough to even explain how inadequate I am. And He loans me His strength to get the job done. Again.

The difference between us is profound. I'm a baby acting like a superhero. He's…a Superhero. But He doesn't mock me for it. He loves me. How did I get so blessed?

How did *we* get so blessed? ⸻ Cynthia

TODAY'S PRAYER

Lord, thanks. Thanks for not laughing in my face
when I flex my ridiculously underdeveloped muscles.
Thank You for standing ready to provide the strength
I need when I wise up enough to ask for it.

Are We There Yet?

Evildoers do not understand what is right,
but those who seek the LORD understand it fully.

PROVERBS 28:5

You know that old adage about there being a joy in the journey? I've never really been a fan of the journey, myself. I'm the girl who wants to take the expressway rather than the side streets. Even if the scenery is staggering, I almost always want to get to my destination as quickly as possible. I'm known for being impulsive, for making decisions quickly. But since it's in our weaknesses that God becomes strong, it is no surprise that, through testing my general impatience, the Lord has presented the greatest teachable moments of my life.

"It's not about the destination," my friend Carol used to tell me. "It's about the journey along the way."

I don't think I realized how wise her words really were. In fact, I remember thinking at the time that she should write greeting cards. But despite the fact that God does sometimes work suddenly, immediately, or instantly, He most often delivers the deepest truths through a process—a series of twists and turns, mountaintops and deep valleys that lead—often slowly—to the end result.

I've had more than a few broken hearts in my life, and I suppose there was a time when I wished I could erase every instance of a bad relationship or poor choice. One particular person comes immediately to mind. He was that one guy—the one in every woman's life—where I lost sight of myself in his shadow, where I behaved in ways I never could have imagined. It took me several years of heartache and craziness, praying for God to transform him, before I finally saw the light.

God wasn't going to change him because he didn't want to be changed. At last, I understood the role that free will plays in the realities of life.

I'm smarter about relationships because of him. I haven't had my heart broken again, at least not to that degree. I can spot a lie more easily now, and I'm much quicker to listen to that still, small voice when it tells me to run like the wind. And the thing is…none of those lessons would have been learned without *Him*.

Whether a wound to the heart, disease to the body, or agony of the mind, it's always a bit of a journey toward ultimate healing, and God's grace is most certainly always involved. How else would we bear the process; how else could we make it through to the end where the lesson is finally counted as learned?

Okay, so I, Sandie Bricker, do hereby admit that there really is a joy to the journey. Maybe it's even more about the journey than about the destination. I don't like it, just to be clear. But I have at least learned something. ⌒ Sandie

TODAY'S PRAYER
. . . .

Lord Jesus, thank You for the lessons that You
patiently teach over time. Help me today to enjoy
the scenery for a change, to pay attention to the bumps
in the road—not so I can jump over them, but so I can
remember where they are if I pass this way again.

A Tough Pill to Swallow

Come and hear, all you who fear God;
let me tell you what he has done for me.

PSALM 66:16

Would you rather be right, or would you rather be happy?"
It's a question that has plagued mankind since, well, the beginning of mankind. From the cradle, it seems, the main goal in life is to "be" happy:

Fresh diaper? Happy baby!

Shiny new trike? Happy toddler!

Driver's license? Happy teen!

Clean room? Happy mom!

Full college scholarship? Happy dad!

We tell ourselves it doesn't take much to make us happy, but woe to the traffic light that turns red when we're late or the thoughtless driver whose fast-food wrapper ends up in our front yard. Someone in the 15-or-less-line put 17 items on the belt? Unacceptable! And I'm every bit as guilty as anyone else of the back-and-forth between happy and not happy, as evidenced by my last sinus infection:

One call to my doctor and, voila, I had an appointment. Color me happy!

But on the way there, I got stuck in traffic. Not so happy.

Found a parking space right in front of the door. Hap–hap–happy!

But I found standing-room-only in the waiting room. <sigh>

Nurse invited me into the exam room on time. Yay!

But it took nearly an hour before the doctor came in. <groan>

Got to the drugstore in record time. Ta-da!

But a computer crash had deleted me from the system. <grrr>

"Oh, well," said I, hoping my smile would erase the pharmacy tech's frown. It did not. I fanned Blue Cross cards across the counter, wondering why *she* was in such a snit. Wasn't me who crashed the system. I had truth (i.e., insurance identification) on my side. Maybe I should point out to her that the customer is always right!

That's when I remembered the old "walk a mile in her shoes" adage. The drugstore chain wrote up the rules and expected her to follow them, whether the customer was sweet or sour, wrong or right. Which reminded me of Moses' no-nonsense "obey!" approach to those stone tablets...and the fact that it was the supreme sacrifice of *Jesus* that delivered grace unto us all.

Now my little dilemma seemed petty and ridiculous. I took a deep breath. I said a prayer for the poor girl—and whatever had put her into a foul mood—and set about helping her to believe that *she* was in the "right." Suddenly she was smiling, fingers click-clacking over the keyboard in a mad search to get me "reinstated." In no time I was home, happily chasing my first dose of antibiotic with a tall glass of water.

Sadly (pun intended), that's life, isn't it? At the end of every day, if we can count up more good things than bad, we're happy. Or at least satisfied.

And that beats "being right" all the way to the drugstore and back! ⌐ Loree

TODAY'S PRAYER

"Ask and you will receive" is but one of thousands of promises
You have made to Your children, Lord. And, oh, ask we do,
for health and peace and prosperity, for ourselves and those
we hold dear. Shower me with Your grace, Father,
that I will find happiness simply by leaving
the "right" things at the foot of the cross.

What Did I Miss?

So we fix our eyes not on what is seen,
but on what is unseen, since what is seen is temporary,
but what is unseen is eternal.

2 CORINTHIANS 4:18

I'm a bookaholic, so one of my favorite things to do is to listen to recorded versions of novels while I drive. I got into the habit after reading Stephen King's *On Writing*. He encourages novelists to read as much fiction as possible, and he says a large percentage of his own reading happens while he travels or jogs, thanks to recorded books. I'm totally onboard with that now, and I no longer mind long drives or traffic jams (not much, anyway), because I know I'll get deep into the world of the novel while I'm on the road.

Although I've never found it difficult to pay attention to my driving while I listen, I have noticed on occasion that my mind will wander from the story. When that happens, I'm forced to rewind and refocus. When I do that, I'm often shocked at how much storyline I missed. It passed me by while I drove and thought about my grocery list or something minor that happened recently or even some tangent triggered by something the book "said."

The other day, the heroine wrote a letter to a soldier who'd said he wanted to marry her, but she didn't hear back from him. Before I realized it, my mind had trailed off to the movie I watched several nights prior, *The Notebook*, because of the hidden-letters facet of that story, which made me think about the star, Ryan Gosling. By the time I finished remembering the crime drama he had made with Sir Anthony Hopkins, my recorded book had moved far into the heroine's story, even referring to people whose introductions I had missed.

Now, there was nothing wrong with my mental wanderings. They were temporary, harmless bits of cerebral fluff. And I still had the book on disc and was able to backtrack and absorb what was permanently etched there. But it occurred to me that I sometimes do the same thing on a spiritual level.

My heavenly Father is so gracious, He makes himself available to me twenty-four hours a day. Whenever I think of Him and His love and guidance and promises, or when I go to Him with praises and petitions, He's there for me, despite everything He has on His plate. While the things of this world will come and go, He'll *always* be there for me.

Is that why I sometimes take my mind off Him for long stretches of time? Is that why I give inordinate attention to what is seen—what is worldly—and sometimes far too little of my attention to what is eternal? Sometimes I catch myself getting all wrapped up in something that honestly doesn't matter in the grand, eternal scheme of things. Sometimes I need to stop, rewind, and refocus—on Him. — Trish

TODAY'S PRAYER

God in heaven, You created this amazing world for us
and created an even more amazing, supernatural world
that I yearn to see. Please help me to live a right life
in this world while I fix my eyes on what matters
eternally, Lord. I pray this in Your gracious name.

Facing Forward

"Forget the former things; do not dwell on the past."
ISAIAH 43:18

It happens whether you're in a canoe or a station wagon. If you face backward, you'll have a view. It just won't help you on your journey.

In my childhood, at a time when my four siblings and I fought epic battles for the primo window seats, we were thrilled when our parents bought a station wagon, offering that wide panoramic view from the back-facing seat. We called it the "way very back." It could hold three of us across.

"Can I sit in the way very back?"

"Me too?"

"Me too?"

"Me— Aww! I get dibs next time."

"Me too!"

What was so fascinating about facing backward, having no clue where we were going but a clear vision of where we'd been?

Why does that still capture our attention?

A friend of the family made several visits to the local prison…as an inmate. He was given multiple opportunities for a fresh start. But he was pointing backward, his attention captivated by where he'd been, the mistakes he'd made, the shame and misery he'd known, the misery he'd caused.

God's grace being what it is, our friend's been given another opportunity for a fresh start. This time feels different to him and to us. Why? He's facing forward this time. He has a clear view of the future, a plan for how to navigate the obstacles ahead—obstacles he would have backed into and tripped over if he'd been facing the other direction.

My husband and I have canoed the complicated web of lakes and rivers in the Canadian wilderness several times. Not recently, though. I told him I could only manage a trip like that once a decade. It's been eighteen years. One of these days he's bound to do the math.

When paddling past small granite islands and long stretches of northwoods forest in the wilderness, we'd get into serious trouble if we tried to find our way facing backward. Could we see interesting scenery that way? Oh, sure. But we'd bash the canoe into rocks, get caught by rogue waves, hit the rapids at the wrong angle, miss our put-in points for portages or a place to camp, and risk remaining constantly lost.

As a child, I soon found that facing backward was a good way to invite car sickness too. I relinquished my dibs on the way very back. I needed to face where we were heading to keep my equilibrium.

I don't think I'm alone.

Making every dance move backward and in heels might have worked for Ginger Rogers when she danced with Fred Astaire, but it's a clumsy way to try to navigate life.

We need to *know* where we've been. But *facing* that direction can invite life sickness. ⸺ Cynthia

TODAY'S PRAYER

Lord, take me by the shoulders and turn me to face the way
You're going. Use the past to propel me forward but not
to consume my attention. Hold my focus on what lies ahead
as I look to and lean on You. No set of rapids is as threatening
as the one I don't see coming, the one I'm not braced for. I'm
grateful You put my past behind You. Help me to do the same.

My Cross to Bear?

Therefore, in order to keep me from becoming conceited,
I was given a thorn in my flesh, a messenger of Satan, to torment me.
Three times I pleaded with the Lord to take it away from me.
But he said to me, "My grace is sufficient for you,
for my power is made perfect in weakness."

2 CORINTHIANS 12:7–9

I was almost ten pounds when I was born (so sorry, Mom). By the third grade, I'd developed a weight problem, and I've been struggling with it ever since. I've tried every diet known to mankind, every pill, juice, shake, bar, vitamin, and injection…I've bought treadmills, bicycles, thigh masters, butt masters, balance balls, weights, bands, and workout DVDs…I've talked to therapists, priests, reverends, personal trainers, nutrition experts, and hypnotists. At the age of fifty-*cough* years old, I am still overweight. What's up with that?!

If I had a nickel for every prayer in which I'd pleaded with the Lord to show me, guide me, lead me, or just miraculously heal me, I would be writing this from that Pacific Ocean beach house I dream about so frequently! The thing that's really strange to me about this lifelong struggle is that I'm a true believer. I have faith for things that other people laugh off. I believe in the promises of God, and I call upon them often. So why is this *one issue* so unattainable?

Someone I love and respect very much told me something not so long ago that's really stayed with me. "You know, Sandie, you have to stop second-guessing God's will. All you can do is the best you can. Beyond that, you have to remember that everything about you was planned before you were even a twinkle in your birth dad's eye. Nothing about you is an accident. You were created with a specific purpose, and what you consider to be your greatest weakness could turn out to be the thing that God uses to drive you forward."

That night, I received a message with today's Scripture verse typed into the body of the e-mail. Nothing else, just the verse, and it really made me take a serious look over my life and the many successes and failures I've had with my weight. Although I'm certainly not willing to accept defeat, I do perceive a certain wisdom in what my friend had to say.

I still have a clear vision of myself in skinny jeans and stiletto boots one day (Hey! Don't judge. I've been carrying this picture since the eleventh grade). And I'm not letting it go until about twenty minutes after I take my final breath. But if I don't manage to attain it before then, there are three things I know for certain: 1) His grace is sufficient for me; 2) in my weakness, He becomes even stronger; and 3) the grapefruit diet wasn't meant to be followed for more than a week. It does unpleasant things to the digestive system beyond that. I'm just sayin'. ⸺ Sandie

TODAY'S PRAYER
· · · · · · · · · · · · · · · · · · ·

Thank You for the grace You offer me that is always sufficient, always enabling, and always arrives tucked into Your beautiful love. When I'm tempted to lament the "accidents" and "curses" that inhabit my life, help me to remember that my weakness invites Your strength.

Mercy Me!

Surely your goodness and love will follow me all the days of my life,
and I will dwell in the house of the LORD forever.

PSALM 23:6

Every now and then, when I'm home alone or wandering the house in the middle of the night, I get that creepy-crawly, "somebody's following me" sensation. Especially when climbing stairs. (When I use the phrase "tuck and run," you can bet I know what I'm talking about!)

The other day, in a mad rush to outrun the…what*ever* it was…I thought of my friend's daughter, recently diagnosed with SAD (Seasonal Affective Disorder). Poor Barbie! Rainy days really get the poor kid down. As part of her treatment, Barbie's mom had to buy a goose-necked lamp and a pricey bulb that mimics sunlight. Yet even when coupled with psychotherapy and medication, cloudy weather and the creepy-crawlies go hand in hand for Barbie.

By contrast, I often joke that I squint because, like Clint Eastwood, I'm sensitive to bright light. See, I really *like* the hush that falls over the land at night, wrapping around me like a soft shadow. Then why, you ask, do I try to outrun it?

Maybe for the same reason so many of us have trouble knowing when to say "The End." Songwriters, poets, authors—we all face this little life dilemma from time to time: Barbie, when the sun hides behind the clouds; high-school sweethearts, when one has outgrown the other; me, when I'm alone, on the stairs, in the darkened house.

It hasn't been all that long since my full-blooded Italian aunt faced the end of her life. Just weeks after she'd blown out the candles on her seventieth birthday cake, the doctors said "terminal." Chemo, radiation, pills, they insisted, would give her a year or so to get her affairs in order.

"Thanks to my lawyer, my accountant, and my financial advisor," she announced, "my affairs couldn't *be* in better order. And," she went on to say, "I've already hired the harpist who'll pluck out 'Amazing Grace' at the funeral and the piper who'll play my favorite Irish ballads at the 'after dinner.'"

Friends and family rallied round, trying to change her mind. "We'll miss you!" they insisted, and "You've got to fight this!" "God will heal you," they cried, "if only you ask Him to."

Her face lit up with the joy of acceptance as she drew them close. "I won't become one of those people who live like they're being chased by the shadow of death. I've lived a good, long life, and soon, I'll live for eternity in paradise!"

So next time I'm alone, on the stairs, in the dark, and that "somebody's following me" sensation tempts me to tuck and run, I'll face and embrace it and call it by name:

Dear, sweet Mercy, my 100 percent Italian auntie. ⌐ Loree

TODAY'S PRAYER
· · · · · · · · · · · · · · · · · · · ·

Dear heavenly Father, when life looks dark and scary
and it seems as though the sun wants to hide forever behind
the clouds, remind me of dear aunt Mercy, who believed
so deeply in Your promise of eternal life and knew that
"The End" for her was, instead, her invitation to bask
in the light of Your glory, evermore. Praise be Your holy name!

When We Think
No One Is Watching

Even small children are known by their actions,
so is their conduct really pure and upright?

PROVERBS 20:11

My adult daughter is my best friend and someone I hold in great admiration. But for the first ten years of her life, she didn't have the benefit of parents who followed Christ and His teachings. When I gave my heart to the Lord, it wasn't clear to my ten-year-old girl that she should do the same. As a matter of fact, it was another eight years before she made that decision.

As a consequence of my early negligence, we had some catching up to do in the discipline-and-teaching department. Although my daughter always had a sweet heart, she gave me a run for my money during her tween and teen years. I tried to be a good example of honest living for her, but I was working against some mighty powerful influences in her life, and she was forever getting into trouble. Sometimes I wondered how so many other parents managed to get their kids to follow the rules. It seemed as if my efforts were futile.

With more than a small degree of trepidation, I allowed her to participate in a two-week foreign exchange program through her high school when she was seventeen. During the trip she lived with a family in Scotland, as did about twenty of her classmates. It wasn't until they returned home that we parents heard about some trouble stirred up across the pond. I learned that my girl and her best friend—or as I called her, her partner in crime—were the only two students who didn't get drunk and carouse around the village, bringing shame upon themselves, their school, and their parents. Every student but my daughter and her partner in crime were suspended from school for a week once they returned to the States.

My daughter's theory was that all of the other students went as wild as they truly were as soon as they were free from their parents' close watch. That could have explained their bad behavior, but it didn't explain my daughter's good behavior (not that I was complaining). As that year progressed, I saw other changes in the choices my daughter made. It didn't all happen at once, but eventually her conduct reflected more than maturity. It reflected a changing heart.

Maybe my efforts weren't so futile after all. And certainly God wasn't ignoring what was going on.

Despite the seemingly upright behavior of my daughter's classmates while they were home and strictly supervised, they became infamous—for a while, at least—because of their unruly actions when left to their actual lack of self-discipline. While I feared my daughter would never clean up her act, she was actually learning through consequences how best to live once she was on her own.

We can profess to be pure and upright, but what do our actions say? ⌁ Trish

TODAY'S PRAYER

. . . .

Dearest Jesus, You know my innermost thoughts and feelings.
You know my weaknesses and how I want my actions
to reflect a loving, gracious heart. Please keep my heart
and my thoughts sweet, charitable, and kind.
Please let me and my children be known as pure
and right because our actions portray us so.

Change of Heart

"My heart is changed within me; all my compassion is aroused."
HOSEA 11:8

I had a change of heart.

My girlfriend and I sat at a local restaurant sipping iced tea and waiting for our taco salads. Conversation never waned between the two of us when we met for lunch. Happy talk. Intriguing ideas. Always a celebration of what the Lord had been doing in our lives lately.

As we chatted, a young family entered the restaurant. I watched them cross the room: a too-young mom, a too-young dad (I wondered if they were married), two toddlers, and an infant. Writers are trained to be observant, so I didn't for a minute think myself judgmental in noticing that their clothes were probably from the thrift shop's clearance rack. They took a table near our booth. I could watch without staring.

They sat the toddlers in booster seats and plopped the baby into a high chair.

Three children already. At their age.

The dad wore ratty jeans and an almost-white T-shirt with…with a pack of cigarettes rolled into the sleeve.

I caught myself before a *tsk* escaped my mouth. Maybe it was a product of that writer-imagination thing, but I pictured those poor babies sucking secondhand cigarette smoke into their fragile little lungs. And could the parents afford better shoes for those children if Dad quit the habit? What other bad habits threatened their family's ability to pay their bills? Did he even have a job?

The waitress took their order while I reined my attention to the discussion around my own table.

But then, the young dad reached for the pack in his sleeve. Right there in the restaurant! I didn't realize I even had any ire, but there it was, popping out as I watched him pull the pack free from his T-shirt sleeve.

A pack of crayons.

He flipped the kids' paper placemats over to the blank side and set a handful of crayons before each of his toddler daughters. Then he picked a marine-blue crayon and began to color a corner of one daughter's sky.

I was so wrong about him. All the ill feelings I'd had about that young man turned into compassion for him and appreciation for a dad who colored with his girls, a dad who told stories, who loved them, who got involved in childcare, and who smiled at their mother while he did so.

My compassion kicked in, tardy and finicky as it was, when I saw the man doing something right.

Where would I be if the Lord acted the way I did? God's compassion for me is constant, not fickle, and kicks in even when my choices turn His stomach.

The Hosea verse that sparked these thoughts says, "All my compassion is aroused" in context with His people consistently choosing to ignore what He told them and reject what He offered. Even *then* His compassion is stirred. Unlike mine.

Remembering that day in the restaurant humbles me. A pack of crayons showed me how far I have to go in understanding what it means to live a life of grace. ⟶ Cynthia

TODAY'S PRAYER

. . . .

Lord who loves perfectly, I'm amazed by You.
Forgive me for being so slow to learn to love like You do.

Love Covers
a Multitude of Sins

The LORD bestows favor and honor;
no good thing does he withhold from those
whose walk is blameless.

PSALM 84:11

Before her untimely death, I'd known Roanne since we were kids. She played such an integral and life-altering role in the person I am now. For instance, she was the first person to believe in me as a writer. And she introduced me to several of the great loves in my life, such as English Breakfast tea, Cary Grant movies, and the difference between Taco Bell and *authentic* Mexican cuisine. That being said, she and I couldn't possibly have been more different.

Very much a Renaissance woman, Roanne's diverse interests included a passion for needlework. She embroidered some of the most stunning canvases, and I often marveled at her ability to sit in a chair for hours on end, focusing on one teeny little stitch after another—especially in contrast with her complete *inability* to focus on any other area of her life in order to complete a task from beginning to end! Eventually those little specks of thread blended together to create something exquisite and astonishing.

My one and only embroidery experience dated back to the summer (and fall and winter) of 1971 when I made a truly awful piece for my mother that she later displayed proudly. But watching Roanne inspired the ridiculous idea that I wanted to give it another go. Roanne threw her enviable enthusiasm and patience into the task of teaching me, and it didn't take long to discover that time had not developed any new skills in me. I still had absolutely no talent whatsoever for embroidery.

After countless hours of work on a Scripture sampler, I threw the canvas down on the ottoman and exclaimed, "I'm so over this!" Roanne set down her own project and encouraged me to pick it up again. "Look at it!" I cried. "It's a mess. There's a whole line of stitches in the wrong color, and look at this one right here!"

Holding it a few feet away, she said, "Now look at it. Do you see the mistakes from there?" I had to admit that I didn't. "There isn't a single wrong stitch that ruins the overall picture," she pointed out. "The only thing that can do that is if you give up and don't finish. It's kinda like how your sins are covered over by what the Lord has already done. The only thing that messes up grace is if you fail to reach out for it."

Roanne always said things like that. But in this particular case, I didn't roll my eyes because she'd actually reached me. Success!

I finished that project after all, quoting her grace reference in my head the whole way to completion. I framed it and hung it on the wall, and I often gazed at it from across the room, knowing full well where to find each mistake but unable to actually see them…and feeling really, really blessed that, in God's perspective, I looked like that sampler.
— Sandie

TODAY'S PRAYER

Thank You, Lord, for looking at the big picture of me
rather than stripping back the grace and redemption
You've given me to cover all the ugly mistakes.

Walking with Grandpa

"I the LORD do not change."

MALACHI 3:6

On the day my Italian grandfather became a US citizen, he bought himself a pocket watch. As he was a foreman at a mattress factory, it came in handy, timing his team's productivity to ensure a few extra dollars in their pay envelopes. Mostly, every *tick-tock* reminded him that he was now a free man. He timed our walks using that watch, too, a tradition that never altered, even on cold, snowy days.

Once, as we maneuvered the slanting, cracked sidewalks of his neighborhood, he told me about his papa's bull. Everyone walked a wide berth around the monster that even brawny men agreed was the stuff children's nightmares are made of. But the animal worked hard, dutifully pulling heavy wagons, grinding wheat and corn to help fill the Citeroni family coffers. Grandpa was twelve—my age—when he got distracted while pouring feed into the beast's trough…and it gored him. Lifting his shirtsleeve, Grandpa showed me the ropelike scar that crisscrossed a hollow of still-missing muscle.

Not long after he told me that story, Grandpa had a stroke. He called me from the hospital and struggled to say, "I won't be home for a while, so will you do me a favor and wind my watch?"

I was proud that he'd trust me with it and only too happy to agree.

"Promise me something?"

"Anything," I said, meaning it.

"Don't ever change, and always remember…you are my heart, *cara mia.*"

I pretended not to understand that he was saying good-bye, and I spent the next week focused on homework, my crush-of-the-week,

Jimmy Cicotti, and caring for the precious timepiece. I loved the job. And I hated it. Because I wanted Grandpa to come home and wind it *himself.*

The following Sunday after services, the hospital called: Grandpa was gone. During those next days, the house filled with friends and family, pies and casseroles, plants and favorite "Frank stories." The days became weeks, and the weeks turned into months, yet I didn't cry for my best friend, my hero, my beloved Grandpa; if that first tear fell, would it be like Noah's ark all over again?

Like Grandpa's dependable watch, life ticked on. I moved east, fell in love, got married, and had kids. Then, recently, on a sunny spring afternoon, the mailman delivered a brown-wrapped package. Inside, nestled on a cloud of tissue paper, was his watch. "Your grandpa would want you to have it," Nonna wrote, days before her own passing.

Of all the treasures I've collected, Grandpa's watch is my most prized possession—despite its $50 appraisal—for it's a reminder of his love and loyalty that inspired such affection that, thirty years after his death, Nonna went to her grave still his devoted widow.

Someday, he will greet me in paradise, but until then, when life is bleak and burdensome, I need only to see that familiar shimmer of gold and hear the dependable *tick-tock* and I'm an innocent girl again…walking with Grandpa. ↬ Loree

TODAY'S PRAYER

Lord of all, I thank You for those precious years and
the treasured memories they evoke. Keep me ever aware that
Your love is far, far more dependable than Grandpa's watch,
as unchanging as its steady *tick-tock.*

Sweet Words

Gracious words are a honeycomb,
sweet to the soul and healing to the bones.

PROVERBS 16:24

One Christmas, a middle-aged relative—we'll name him Ted—gave everyone in the family the DVD of a stand-up comic's live performance. He loved the comedian's routine and wanted to share it with everyone.

I'm no prude. I was grown up, with a lifetime's worth of worldly experiences, by the time I found Christ. So I've heard and seen what "the world" finds humorous. I can handle bawdy humor, and I love wry, satirical storytelling.

But this guy's words were far from honeycomb sweetness. He wasn't even funny, just foul and juvenile.

Later I heard that Ted lost his temper with my aging mom after he played the same DVD in front of her and she reacted with confused shock at the content. That didn't sit well with me.

So at the next family gathering, when we all sat down to a meal and Ted started to talk about this same comic, I interrupted. "Ugh! I *hate* that guy!"

That news didn't sit well with Ted. Especially not delivered as it was, in front of everyone to whom he had given the DVD. He seethed during our before-meal prayer, uttering expletives and breathing heavily. Then he wolfed down his meal and stormed out of the room.

This paints a harsh picture of Ted—there's no other way to paint him in this instance. But the point of this story isn't to focus on Ted or the vulgar comedian. It is to focus on *moi*.

"Ugh! I *hate* that guy!" Not exactly sweet words. No images of honey spring to mind, do they? I felt justified in taking a stance against the comedian's words and in squelching a rehash of his humor in mixed company. But my method was far from pleasant.

Clearly, Ted felt that a part of his identity was connected to this DVD because he had made it a gift to others. What he probably heard was, "Ugh! I hate *you*." I'm not saying that's a healthy or mature reaction on his part. I'm saying it's the likely one.

Had I taken the time to find a kinder way to express my thoughts, Ted might still have taken it personally. But that really isn't the issue here. My role as a Christian is to find words that fall sweetly on the ears of others, whenever I can.

I often picture the stereotypical, sweet-talking Christian woman whose voice is as soft as bunny tails, whose delivery is what you'd expect from a cuddly lamb, if it could talk. She is *so* not me, and I sometimes think of women like that as kind of…weak.

My voice is often more like a crow's, my delivery like a snapping turtle's. I'd have to work hard to sound that pleasant, which is probably what those "weak" women have already figured out. ⌐ Trish

TODAY'S PRAYER

Father God, You give us the perfect example of how
we should tailor our speech when we address others.
Please remind me of that, Lord, when I choose to add
my two cents to a conversation. Help me to stop
and think about how my words reflect You
and Your precious Son. Please make my words,
whatever their message, as pleasant as honey.

Skinny Fingers

For the law was given through Moses;
grace and truth came through Jesus Christ.

JOHN 1:17

I have to celebrate my hands."

Far from a narcissistic declaration, when those words came out of my daughter's mouth, we both knew we were witnesses to a profound insight.

We know what it means to "struggle with our weight," which sounds like wrestling a sweaty sumo guy for permission to breathe. Okay, that's a better analogy than I thought it was going to be.

Carbs like us too much. They stalk us, crave a little time with us, beg until we let them rent space on our hips. But we've both set our minds to eat healthier and no longer grab food unthinkingly (as often) or for all the wrong reasons—emotional ache, paper cut, first day of spring… I've decided to let vegetables dominate my dinner plate. Daughter Amy has shown remarkable discipline in cutting calories. We're far from where we want to be. But we recognize the importance of acknowledging small victories.

We still don't like our chins. Any of them. But Amy's thrilled that her hands look different. Her fingers are slim. Noticeable progress. *Slim* isn't a word that works its way into daily conversation in our family. I had to look it up to make sure I spelled it correctly. Amy's fingers are slim.

Mine look trimmer too. My wedding rings slop around freely as opposed to lodging in that fleshy ditch where they've lived so long.

We still have enough excess to make us good candidates for being marooned on a desert island for a good chunk of time without any danger of our bikinis falling off (yeah, like we'd wear bikinis), but we're celebrating small victories on our way to the larger ones. Dropping a size. Buttoning a jacket. Having to belt a once-tight pair of slacks.

What does that observation have to do with John 1:17?

Freedom.

The closer we come to our health goals, the more we recognize the difference between where we were and where we want to be.

The law God gave through Moses showed us where we ought to be and how utterly impossible it was to get there without the promised Messiah. The grace and truth that came through Christ brought us the freedom of possibility, the joy of progress, and the hope of growing to reflect Him rather than our former selves.

When I'm tempted to mourn the fact that, spiritually, I still have more than enough chins, I'm going to take a closer look at what's different in me because of Jesus. What's gone, conquered, reined in, trimmer because of Him?

At one time, I would have shared a tidbit of gossip. I would have stormed off if someone offended me. I used to skirt the truth when filling in the "weight" question on my driver's license renewal. Even before vegetables, God and I conquered that temptation. I remember when I'd say I would pray but never follow through. Small victories.

My fingers are slimmer. I have to celebrate my hands. — Cynthia

TODAY'S PRAYER

Lord of all, I worship You. Thank You for understanding my weaknesses and providing the power to overcome them. Thank You for the small victories along the way to larger ones.

Friends in High Places

"Before they call I will answer;
while they are still speaking I will hear."

ISAIAH 65:24

I love me some Diann Hunt! The woman is extraordinary. She's funny, talented, insightful, and such a good friend. In addition to all of that, of course, we share a very unique thread in that we've both battled ovarian cancer and won. When she delivered the news to me recently that her battle was on again, I hung up the phone, doubled over, and sobbed for I don't know how long. Before the day was out, I'd posted a message on Facebook telling people I wanted to start a prayer loop on behalf of my friend; anyone interested could e-mail me privately.

A dozen of us took up the flag and let it fly. Before the end of the day, we were praying fervently for Diann. One by one, other people's needs came to light as well, and we began praying about those too. Around two or three in the morning on the second day, I found myself doubled over again—this time in excruciating pain. I was alone. I started vomiting and writhing from the intensity of the pain, and I finally picked up the phone and called an ambulance.

In the emergency room, waiting for the pain medication in my IV to take effect, my thoughts went to Diann and then to the prayer loop. Ten minutes later, I'd sent a message through my best friend to ask them all to pray for me.

There were X-rays and ultrasounds and blood work, all in order to detect kidney stones and a very bad infection that had spread from my bladder to my left kidney. At around ten o'clock that morning, they sent me home. By the time I got there and was settled, even before I took the quiet time to pray on my own, my BlackBerry had filled up with message after message from the loop. All those beautiful prayer warriors had been crying out to the Lord on my behalf for hours.

In the days that followed, there were some complications. I needed more tests, had to see my own doctor, and continued to struggle with feeling better. All the while, the faithful prayers flowed, and I felt their vigor; the grace of it all just engulfed me as I regained my strength during the next week.

I find it so ironic that I'd been the one to spearhead this group of people into a prayer group, and I was the one who benefited from the fruits of their willing spirits. My God had secured and spread out a net beneath me before I ever found myself on the unexpected high wire. And He'd used a phenomenal group of people to do it. What started for the benefit of Diann, and even me, developed into so much more. It's an ongoing support system that reaches far beyond a dozen women who just serve the same loving God. ⟿ Sandie

TODAY'S PRAYER
. . . .

Lord Jesus, my heart runs over with love and awe for You.
Before we even stop praying You're there, listening, loving,
and working out the reply. Each and every day,
You're the help I need before I even know I need it.
You're my own personal rock star!

The Blessings Jar

Brothers and sisters, pray for us that the message of the Lord
may spread rapidly and be honored.

2 THESSALONIANS 3:1

I'm the first to admit that my life is like a big jar overflowing with blessings. Like most Christians, when there's a leak in the jar, I pray. The bigger the leak, the harder I pray, and if it's a really big crack, I ask fellow believers to pray *with* me. Not long ago, when tragedy struck my family, I started the prayer chain with a favorite relative.

Several years earlier, Aunt Kate had been diagnosed with an incurable cancer. Though three rounds of chemo, two more of radiation, all while swallowing experimental drugs, did little more than make her bald and skinny, we lifted her in prayer. After months of suffering, Kate went in for a routine blood test…and the lab found no cancer. Shocked, her oncologist ordered more tests. "There's no sign of cancer," he admitted, "and I have no medical or scientific explanation for the cure."

Who better to ask to join me in prayer than the woman who was the living, breathing, *healthy* recipient of a grace-filled, God-made miracle!

Imagine my surprise when she refused, citing 1 Timothy 2:5–6. "He is *God*," she scolded, "and already knows about your petty problems…*and* will resolve them as He sees fit." By the time we hung up, I could barely read the verse through my tears: "There is one God and one mediator between God and mankind, the man Christ Jesus, who gave himself as a ransom for all people."

I'd read the passage many times, but *my* interpretation led me to believe that the Old Testament practice of sacrificing animals to earn an audience with God ended when Jesus died on the cross. His sacrifice allowed us to stand unashamed before the Father in praise and in prayer, for ourselves *and* on behalf of others. Had I misconstrued the meaning of that verse?

In a word, *no!*

All through the Bible, we find reference after reference, encouraging believers to pray in agreement about individual and community concerns. Asking others to join us in prayer is an act of humility that allows God to accomplish things we could never achieve as individuals. The apostle Paul understood this only too well and repeatedly asked people to pray for him.

The Almighty tells us to serve one another, and one of the best ways we can do that is to pray for them *and with them.*

By the grace of God, Aunt Kate is still cancer-free. And the petty problem I brought to her that day, years ago? I'm happy to report that it's solved and (almost) forgotten!

"How wide and long and high and deep is the love of Christ"!

〜 Loree

TODAY'S PRAYER
. . . .

Thank You, Father. My eyes fill with tears each time I
remember that the gift of Your grace is just that...a gift.
I am humbled that through grace I am saved, reborn, given
new life—here and in heaven—and all You ask in return is that
I receive it by faith. O Lord, I do believe. I thank You for loving
me, even when I'm unlovable. Fill me with Your Spirit
and help me to live for You, now and forever.

Sharing Blessings

The generous will themselves be blessed,
for they share their food with the poor.
PROVERBS 22:9

It's been a few decades since I worked in Washington, DC, and there are so many things about being in the city that I miss. I truly love my current status, which enables me to work from home sweet home, but I also loved the active, noisy, bustling environment inherent in working "a good job in the city," as Tina Turner would say.

I'm sure the situation is worse today than it was twenty years ago, but one of the constants of my time in the city was the appearance of homeless people on the streets. Workers dashed from place to place and became jaded to the sight and smell of scraggly men wearing cocoons of dingy gray blankets, huddling over grates in the sidewalk, seeking warmth. On occasion, the homeless panhandle. As often as not, though, they simply sit there, thinking who knows what. Many are mentally challenged, many are addicts, all are a little scary at first and sad always.

Because of the "scary" part, I tended to be one of those people rushing by. I was busy, and I was usually only on the street to grab some lunch to take back to the office. One weekend, though, I worked overtime with a coworker. We got to the office early and neither of us had had breakfast, so we crossed the street to pick up some MacSomethings. We walked past the obligatory homeless man on the way, and neither of us said anything about that.

But when my friend ordered her breakfast, she ordered a second one as well. She answered my teasing by saying, "Oh, no, this is for the man outside." I was immediately convicted. That thought had never occurred to me. I'd always been cautioned not to give money to the homeless, because chances were likely they'd spend it on whatever substance they were addicted to, so I was aiding their demise. But this was genius.

My friend allowed me to split the cost of the man's breakfast, and I couldn't believe how joyful it felt to be a tiny part of making his day just a little less horrible.

The catch was that I wasn't always on the way to buying food when I passed homeless people. Finally, the Lord convicted me further: it's really not my business what a poor man does with what I give him. That's between him and God.

So I developed the habit of carrying a few dollars in my pocket whenever I left the office. Again, I felt immediate and amazing joy with the simple gesture of handing a bill or two to someone, whether he asked for it or not, and saying, "God bless you." When someone from the office accompanied me, my action often sparked conversations about charity, the homeless, and God. I don't know how many people the Lord touched through those conversations, but they were conversations we wouldn't have had if I hadn't given away a few measly dollars. And my actions came about from my coworker's sharing food with the poor. Blessings grow like that. ⟶ Trish

TODAY'S PRAYER

Dearest Jesus, every cent I own belongs to You.
Please help me to remember that
and to give freely to Your children in need.

Whether Vain

As God's co-workers we urge you not to receive God's grace in vain.

2 CORINTHIANS 6:1

Something in me rattled like a rock in the clothes dryer when I heard that a school system several states away had decided to eliminate cursive writing from its curriculum. The reason?

"Our students' time can be better spent learning computer skills rather than cursive."

It's not that I'd argue the point. But do I want to walk into a museum and hear the curator say, "And in this exhibit, a quaint and at one time artistic form of written communication called *cursive*. In its declining years, it served a purpose for signatures until the discovery that a squiggly line would work just as well. A real find for our museum, in this glass case is a rare, perfectly preserved antiquity—a handwritten note."

My fingers spend an inordinate amount of time on a computer keyboard and very little gripping a pen or pencil. But I remember learning cursive in school. The rhythm. The angles. The loops and swirls and careful placement of the dot above an *i* and the cross member of a lowercase *t*.

One of my most cursive-conscious teachers (some would call her obsessed) seemed determined to create a room of students with identical signatures. She insisted we purchase special pens that forced us to conform to her idea of the ideal grip. I wonder how she'd feel about people who talk with their thumbs? *R u cmg 2 prty? C u.*

What was I thinking when creating that texting example? No one uses capital letters anymore.

In her classroom, Mrs. Strictandproudofit's students learned new vocabulary words every week. Important words like *omnibus. Logorrhea. Phrontistery.*

We also were required to keep one notebook of "Homonyms" and another for "Palindromes." I capitalized those two titles because they were written in cursive on the front covers of our notebooks. Fascinating stuff. No, really, it was…for word nerds like me.

I have that teacher to thank for helping me create future magazine article, book, and devotional titles using homonyms. *The Rain of the King. Knot on My Watch. Be Stings.*

Subtle regional differences in the way we pronounce words open new possibilities. *Weather vane. Weather vain. Weather vein. Whether vain.*

A few months ago, I took a serious look at a Scripture verse I'd skimmed past. "We urge you not to receive God's grace in vain." A "whether vain" verse.

What does it mean to receive God's grace in vain? To waste it?

I know some people like that. They heard about the grace God offers through His Son Jesus, expressed momentary appreciation—at an altar, kneeling beside their bed, bent over a Bible—but then abused that gift of grace. Some neglected to feed their faith and it starved to death. Some neglected to protect it and it was battered by winds of circumstance. Some ignored it, thinking it was fine for that moment in time but not for the long haul.

The price was the same for Jesus no matter how the gift was handled later. Lord, I want to treat it with the respect and honor it deserves.

⌐ Cynthia

TODAY'S PRAYER

Lord God, help me to prove every day that Your gifts
of grace were not wasted on me.

Divine Purpose
for Dummies

The teaching of the wise is a fountain of life,
turning a person from the snares of death.

PROVERBS 13:14

My brother and his wife are botanists. Terry built a greenhouse for Laurie, and I remember watching her tend her flowers and plants one time while visiting them in Louisiana. Without saying a word, Laurie fully *communicated* with them as she tended to their needs. It was almost a spiritual experience, and I went home to California *inspired!* I planted some seeds, bought a couple of plants…and killed them all within a month.

Send an unruly dog with no manners or self-control to live with me for a month and I'll teach that dog to save Timmy from the well! But plants? Not my gift. So imagine my horror when I opened the door recently to find an enormous plant there to greet me. Sweet sentiment from the sender, but they obviously hadn't received the memo about me.

I quickly moved the massive thing to the backyard patio, and two days later, it had that look that tulips get. No matter what you do for them, tulips tend to wilt quickly, bending to their death—much like the big plant on my patio, sloped down to the ground, dejected and unhappy.

I dumped a bunch of water on it, and the next morning it appeared less unhappy. I moved it out of the direct Florida sunshine, and it thrived a little more. The problem with this scenario is that I am now faced with a daily race to the patio to see what I've done to Luther. (This is what I call it. *Luther.* I don't know why.)

For many years, I've nursed a bit of a grudge about the fact that God chose to make it impossible for me to bear children. The maternal instinct in me is, and always has been, enormous. Kids often follow me around like I'm the Pied Piper; babies always reach for me first; and I've become The Awesome (visiting) Aunt to the children of my closest friends. But still, never one of my own.

The truth is…sometimes I forget to feed my dog. Although Sophie is pretty great at gently reminding me and she's very forgiving once her bowl is full…Luther? Not so much, with his constant moody displays and guilty chastisement when I forget the water. And to compound the matter, people remark when they see him. "What have you *done* to that plant?"

So I now have adopted a daily plan because of Luther: every morning, water the plant (and the dog). Check for direct sunlight (and a full bowl). Now and then, plant food (and doggie treats) are definitely in order. Try not to kill the plant (or the dog).

It came late in life, but I think I'm on to something here. Perhaps God's grace includes an individual plan for each of us. Maybe some of us are meant to be moms and greenhouse owners; others of us, doting family friends who go home to our dogs and silk plants. — Sandie

TODAY'S PRAYER

Help me to be thankful for and excel in those things
You've given me to do and never strive to tackle the tasks
and gifts You've assigned to someone else.

A Thrill a Minute

"What good is it for someone to gain the whole world,
yet forfeit their soul?"

MARK 8:36

When I was a little girl, few things excited me more than when my parents said, "Put on your sneakers and grab your jackets, kids; we're going to the amusement park!" Back then, I was an adventure junkie; the bigger and scarier the ride, the better I liked it. I'm not sure when—or why—it happened, but one day the thrill of hurtling through space turned into white-hot fear, and these days, I can't hang curtains unless the chair I'm standing on is guaranteed not to reel and rock, not even a smidge!

My dream about becoming an author reminds me of one of those roller-coaster rides. The "big idea?" That was me, standing in the "this-author-wants-to-be-published" line, waiting to belt myself into the car. Each *tick-tick-tick* as it climbed to the top of the first hill? *Stage One, Story Development.* Those next ticks? Setting, then character development, point of view, conflict, and dialogue. Those ups and downs earned titles such as *Edits* and *Rewrites* and *Second-Guessing Myself.* That last hill—the steepest and most terrifying of all: *Typing "The End."* And then, the final stomach-churning plummet that made me hold my breath and doubled my heartbeat as I hit the SEND key.

And after exhaling that big gulp of air? Why, I got right back into line, of course, and waited as the editors and agents I'd sent my story to sifted through the people-tall stacks of mail piled on their desks to get to mine. I stared at the phone and watched the mailbox. I read e-mail, but "We'd like to offer a contract!" wasn't among any of the messages.

So I got back into line. Again. And I buckled myself in. Again… despite what my published author friends told me about the types of novels that didn't sell, despite the arduous years they'd poured into writing them. They complained about small publishing houses that were being gobbled up by bigger ones and midsized companies that had gone belly-up. They groaned when editors took extended maternity leave after telling them how much they believed in their stories. They whimpered as bookstore chains folded, whined when distributors stopped distributing. Then agents culled their client lists, and the editors *not* on maternity leave began pulling double-duty, making that long and painful wait between SEND and REPLY take twice as much time as it had before.

I couldn't help but ask: "Is my dream worth all this agony?"

I said a loud and resounding "Yes!"

And whatever *your* dream is, "Yes" should be your answer too. Because whether part or all of your dream comes true, you will have yet another reason to glorify God your Father, who used every up-and-down moment you endured to prove His love…

…and thrill you with the exhilarating gift of His grace. — Loree

TODAY'S PRAYER

. . . .

O God in heaven, I know that You want me to be a conduit
of Your grace so that Your loving-kindness can flow from me
into the lives of those near and around me. Use me, dear Lord,
to pass on the simple truth: though we have not—cannot—
earn it, Your love knows no bounds. Hallelujah!

Singles Only!

There is surely a future hope for you,
and your hope will not be cut off.
PROVERBS 23:18

I have a friend whose husband is sharp and hardworking, who gave his all for the company for which he used to work. He loved his job, and it showed in his dedication to an organization that has since grown to be a huge conglomerate.

There was one catch, though. The founder was relatively young, single, and highly successful, which may have influenced corporate policy. Social events, like company-sponsored trips to Hawaii and elaborate company dinners, while designed purely for pleasure rather than business, were *verboten* for spouses. Married employees were expected to attend as singles at all events.

I would imagine that every one of us knows someone who has been touched by an illicit workplace "romance." They come about strictly as a result of men and women working long hours in close proximity and letting their guards down. Imagine the additional stress in company-sponsored social interaction—sometimes involving several consecutive days of celebrating, vacationing, most assuredly drinking, all away from spouses. Plenty of questionable hijinks went on, as one would imagine. Yes, marriages endure and survive, but would you want yours to have to suffer that temptation?

My friend's husband tended to go along with most of the events, but never comfortably. He was less enthused than others, and in some rare instances, he didn't attend at all. He probably would have seen a more rapid rise within the company had he been a more willing player, but he had his wife and children in mind, and sometimes he simply had to risk his political corporate status in order to uphold honor for his family and his Christian principals.

Today's verse in Proverbs is surrounded by other verses about why one might envy others who seem to do brilliantly well, even though they don't give thought to God or His tenets. We can all fall prey to that kind of envy, especially if we notice the success of nonbelieving people in the same field we're in: *Oh, sure, it's easy for her to do that well! She caters to all the worldly [employers, clients, readers, enterprises].*

Maybe so, but God's Word, above, encourages us by turning our thoughts to future hope. Our hope will not be severed simply because others seem to do so well.

There may be only so many corporate positions to fill, so many awards to win, so many promotions to achieve, or so many readers to gain, but the promises God has in mind specifically for me will be fulfilled regardless of what goes on around me. My part in that plan is to remain hopeful and trust Him to bring about everything that must happen to make that hope a reality.

My friend's husband eventually took a position at another corporation. Better pay, family-friendly, and less stressful. This hope-and-promise stuff is for real! ∾ Trish

TODAY'S PRAYER
. . . .

Thank You, Father, that You remain aware of my efforts
to live a life that conforms to Your commands. Please help me
to remain ever-hopeful and trusting and to turn a blind eye
to the apparent success of those who pursue that success
for different reasons than I pursue mine. And please
help me to remember for whom I do my work.

This Is Grace

In him we have redemption through his blood,
the forgiveness of sins, in accordance with the riches
of God's grace that he lavished on us.

EPHESIANS 1:7–8

My first grandchild entered life on a tsunami of pain. A devastating wave of emotional and spiritual concerns accompanied what should have been a joy-filled announcement—"Mom, we're pregnant."

The words were couched with shame and embarrassment. My son and his girlfriend weren't married and faced far more challenges than the fact that she craved fish sticks and Funyuns. They both knew they'd made bad decisions. One of those "what were we thinking?" decisions meant that now, rather than ironing out their relationship issues and dealing with a 747-worth of baggage, they—and we—prepared for a baby in the house.

As with most parents of young people in trouble, we were heartbroken over their choice to bypass the divine plan for a husband and wife to bring children into the world in God's glorious timing. It's not that we didn't understand how a thing like that could happen. But my husband and I and everyone else concerned knew that the path my son and his girlfriend chose came laced with difficulties and complications they weren't prepared to handle, challenges the Lord never intended them to experience.

The young woman was homeless, and a legal issue kept them from getting married right away. My son had a home of his own a few miles from ours, but the expectant mom lived at our house. As her belly grew, we tamped our disappointment and chose to love and forgive, taking our cue from the mercy that floods the pages of Scripture. Together we walked through morning sickness and fatigue and community stares and whispers. We traversed a path of embarrassment and concern and faced challenges that only happened to "other people." We felt every bit of the baby weight on our own frames and somehow adopted the waves of nausea and the clenching of false labor in our own bodies.

But through it all, we counted on the wonder of the Lord's forgiveness, His redemptive heart, His ability to turn what started out as distressing into something of great beauty. It's what He does. He molds rough clay to make art. He recycles pain to make a place for His joy to land.

As expected, He did just that.

At four thirty in the morning one day in September, my son came to get us from the waiting room to lead us into the birthing center, where a new life had entered the world moments before. Warm and bright-eyed and rose-petal pink, the child was laid into my eager Grammie arms.

"Mom," my humbled but glowing son said, as if a formal introduction were necessary, "this is Grace."

I drew that darling baby to my heart, as I imagine the Lord drew me, and answered, "Yes, it is. *This* is grace." ∽ Cynthia

TODAY'S PRAYER

Father God, how is it that You can make something
so incredibly beautiful out of the messes we give you?
Yet You do. And we're grateful. You don't just forgive,
You lavish the riches of Your grace on us.
Thank you for the exceptional and exceptionally
well-loved child Grace...and for where-would-we-be-
without-it divine grace.

Who, Me?

At this, she bowed down with her face to the ground.
She asked him, "Why have I found such favor in your eyes
that you notice me—a foreigner?"
RUTH 2:10

I adore Ruth! She's one of my favorite Bible friends, for so many reasons, but I really identify with that unassuming, somewhat clueless nature of hers. There she is, extending so much unselfish grace toward Naomi; yet when the Lord touched the heart of Boaz to bless her, Ruth immediately wondered why she'd found favor with him.

Why do we do that?

I love Proverbs 3:4. It says we find favor with both God and man. In fact, it's one of several Scriptures that I've placed where I can see it every day. So you wouldn't think I'd always be so astonished when God's grace glides me through; but like Ruth, despite what I know about the character of God, I'm often taken by complete surprise!

When I was just barely out of my teens, I had a terrible accident and my car was completely demolished. I pried open the door and walked away without a scratch on me. I asked myself so many times: Why had my life been spared that way?

I've recently been dealing with a leg problem that has affected my mobility in sudden and profound ways. During the ordeal, I discovered that I had overlooked the expiration of my driver's license by several months, and the only way to renew it was a trip to the DMV. I made two treks there before I was able to collect all the paperwork they needed for renewal, and both times it was excruciatingly painful for me to stand and wait in the inevitable lines.

On that third and final trip, I sat in my car outside for about ten minutes before going in, praying that I would somehow find the strength to do it one more time. I finally took a deep breath, braced myself for another ordeal, grabbed my cane, and slowly hobbled toward the front door.

A man inside left his place in line to hurry and open the door for me. The woman behind the counter called me directly up to her desk to inspect my paperwork. When she sent me to another area and it was announced that they'd encountered a computer problem and we would have to stand in line until it was resolved, the young man in front of me suddenly broke away, fetched a chair, dragged it toward me, and softly said, "This might be easier for you." I left the DMV less than an hour later with my new license in hand.

I thought of Ruth that morning on the drive home, and I wondered how many times God's favor glides me through a situation and I never have the insight to acknowledge Him. His promises await all His children, and yet so often we fail to recognize the manifestation of His love when it's laid out right before our eyes. — Sandie

TODAY'S PRAYER
. . . .

Thank You, Lord, for making such a beautiful plan that includes
me. Help me to recognize Your hand in every situation
of grace and favor, remembering always the honor
and privilege—and promise!—of being called Yours.

Furry Wings
and Fuzzy Halos

Charm is deceptive, and beauty is fleeting;
but a woman who fears the LORD is to be praised.

PROVERBS 31:30

When my daughters were young, we lived in Maryland farm country, far from the nearest...anything. Once, while driving home from the grocery store, my trusty Nova conked out. In the center lane of a highway. Miles from the nearest exit. With night falling. And snow in the forecast. And three hungry and yawning kids in the back seat. I pumped the gas pedal, but it was no use. The motor refused to turn over.

I ran down my short list of options: hike to the nearest gas station with the girls in tow or hike to my husband's office just past the next exit. "Please, Lord," I whispered, "get us home safely...and get us there *soon*."

At that precise moment, a little red sports car pulled up behind us. Its driver, a flashy middle-aged woman in a long fur coat, jogged closer, holding tight to a thick, fuzzy hat as she squinted into the icy wind. "Oh, sweet Jesus," she exclaimed. "Car trouble?"

The TV news was full of scary stories about carjackings, roadside muggings, missing persons...and in one case, the suspect was <gasp> *a woman!* I cranked down the window, but only an inch. "Yes," I squeaked out.

"Dear Lord...do you park your car outside at night?"

"Yes."

"Probably just a little water in the line," she said. "My husband's a mechanic, and I think I have just what you need in my glove box."

A knife? Maybe even a pistol? I wondered. But before I could speculate on other weapons, she was back and hoisting a can of Drygas. "I'll just pour this into your gas tank and you'll be on your way in no time."

She didn't give me time to object, and when she returned to the window with the empty can, the lady peeked into the backseat and, smiling, waved at the kids. "I can follow you home," she said, "and make sure you all get there safely."

I rooted in my purse and withdrew a five-dollar bill. "No. Thanks. You've done so much alre—"

"You don't owe me a penny. My husband's a mechanic, remember? I get this stuff for free!"" She giggled and then added, "Now, crank 'er up. I said a prayer for you while I was dumping this stuff into the tank. I just know God is watching over you and those beautiful babies of yours."

One turn of the key had the Nova purring like a kitten. Tears of relief filled my eyes as I laughed. "Thank you," I said.

But when I turned, she was gone.

And so was her car.

"Mommy," my youngest said, "I didn't know angels drove tiny red convertibles."

Was the fur-clad woman an angel? Or just a wonderful coincidence?

I won't know until I reach heaven's gates, but I know this: the woman in the matching fur hat and coat will be praised by my family every time it snows! — Loree

TODAY'S PRAYER

Thank You, loving Father, for carrying me through every
trying moment in my life and for turning my fear
and suspicion into calm serenity. You are my shelter
and my Lord, amen and amen!

Seeing the Truth in Time

At the name of Jesus every knee should bow,
in heaven and on earth and under the earth,
and every tongue acknowledge that Jesus Christ is Lord,
to the glory of God the Father.

PHILIPPIANS 2:10–11

When I was a fine young chickadee, full of romantic notions and all kinds of misconceptions about real life and my own capabilities, I fell for a young man with a natural talent for honing in on every vulnerable aspect of my personality. He played the romance card beautifully, and I was sucked right in, regardless of some pretty horrible behavior on his part. With my starry-eyed, naive blessing, he distracted me from accomplishments and goals of which I was fully capable. I pretty much made him my everything.

After a year of this relationship, I was one insecure, confused, mistreated mess. I sought professional counseling and was advised that I had invested far too much of myself in this fellow. I needed to pursue activities and ambitions that had nothing to do with my devotion to him and everything to do with my own independence. "Take some college courses," the counselor said. "Consider hobbies for your own personal enjoyment! Spend time with girlfriends, apart from him, once in awhile."

Of course, at the time, I thought the counselor would have given me different advice had she but known what a catch this guy was. I couldn't risk losing him to another girl by turning my attentions elsewhere.

But the day finally dawned when I realized I had been duped all along. Despite solid, truthful advice, I had carried on my shallow existence, not realizing how much better my life could be. I accepted that the counselor had been right. I had been wrong.

I think of that humble realization when I read today's verse. As a believer in the Lord's gracious gift of salvation, I crave that day when we will enthusiastically kneel right there in His physical presence and acknowledge that He is Lord. Imagine that!

I don't want to be a woman who hears about His grace but chooses to ignore it—who carries on in a shallow life, unaware of how much better life could be. And worst of all, to be kneeling on that day, at the name of Jesus, for sad reasons rather than joyous ones. I look forward to falling to my knees because I'm thrilled, as a believer. Not kneeling in the worst, most painful kind of humiliation possible, knowing I've been wrong all along and have left it too late.

I want that day to be a celebration for everyone I know. I remember the pigheaded young woman I was when very little sound advice got through to me, when I was certain I knew better, even though the truth was buried deep in my heart. If I hope to influence others about the joy, blessing, and absolute necessity of recognizing Jesus for who He is and what He offers, I need to ask for all the help I can get.

⌐ Trish

TODAY'S PRAYER

. . . .

Precious Lord Jesus, I love that one day everyone
will acknowledge You as Lord. In the meantime, I pray
that You'll please help me to live and speak in a way
that will help others recognize You for who You are.

What's That Smell?

Perfume and incense bring joy to the heart,
and the pleasantness of a friend springs from their heartfelt advice.
PROVERBS 27:9

What is that *smell?*"

It wasn't asked with the lighthearted voice of a shopper lured into a candle store by the scent of—*what is that?*—pumpkin-pie spice or cinnamon-apple crisp or brown-sugar pound cake. It wasn't said with a smile and a soul-satisfying deep breath on the edge of an orange grove in full bloom. The scene wasn't a late spring deck where the fragrance of lilacs wafted on one breeze and lily-of-the-valley on the next.

The "fragrance" came from the heat duct in the family room.

Dead mouse?

I know what a dead mouse smells like. You can't live in a hundred-year-old house in the country without developing a nose for that smell. This was different.

A furtive search for the source of the odor turned futile. My beloved and I looked everywhere—on the canning shelves, inside the furnace, under the water heater, in the dark corners of the fieldstone basement that I only venture into if I have no other option. None.

We never did find the culprit. It…and the smell…eventually dissolved or disappeared or, oh, I don't really want to know. I'm just glad it's gone. If it comes back again, we're moving.

While we waited for the odor to dissipate, I thought about my mom. That sounds incredibly rude, and I apologize to moms everywhere. What I mean is that the ability to smell is a gift I don't always appreciate. My mom did…after it was gone.

Congestive heart failure stole her strength, but a bizarre reaction to a medical procedure stole her ability to taste and smell. She missed the smell of lemons and lily-of-the-valley and Baby Magic lotion on a newborn. She missed knowing when the turkey was done by the aroma. When we visited her apartment, she'd pull a quart of milk from her fridge and ask, "Would you sniff this? I can't tell if it's still good." She missed knowing when something had soured.

"Perfume and incense bring joy to the heart," reads Proverbs 27:9. The ability to smell is one of life's great, though underappreciated, joys.

I may whine about the "gift" when an unidentified stink wrinkles my nose. But when I slice into a lemon, I think of how much Mom would have enjoyed that scent.

Buttered popcorn. The air between snowflakes. Fresh basil. Sun-dried pillowcases. Warm brownies. Toasted coconut. Campfire. Jasmine tea.

Joy to the heart. Sticky toffee buns.

I can smell. Eucalyptus. That's a grace-gift (hazelnut coffee) I've taken for granted (lavender) too long. Strawberries. — Cynthia

TODAY'S PRAYER

Father God, how many other grace-gifts of Yours
have I used without fully appreciating them? Most of them.
Give me a new one today—the ability to notice and the good
sense to thank You. That first breath of celestial air must have
smelled so incredible to Mom. I wonder if she noted a whiff
of Old Spice when she found Dad waiting for her there.
Your love overwhelms me on days like today, Lord,
when I realize anew that You gave me everything
I'd need to enjoy everything You created.
May my gratitude reach You as a sweet fragrance.

Missing the Point

It is a trap to dedicate something rashly
and only later to consider one's vows.

PROVERBS 20:25

Y ou really want to help, and so you impulsively blurt out your
plans. "I can lend you the money, Sarah. It will take care of the
immediate situation. Just pay me back whenever you can." And then
reality sets in.

Yes, you have the money in your savings account, but what if
Sarah doesn't repay the debt before the taxes come due? What if the
circumstance is part of God's plan for Sarah's life? Have you stolen the
teaching opportunity by rashly swooping in to help?

My father was a strong and resolute man, an influence over our
family's life that loomed large and cast an imposing shadow. If a decision needed to be made, he made it without flinching. I can't tell you
how many times I found myself in a tight spot only to be rescued by
my father. I learned early what a hero is made of.

The upside: I had someone in my life that I could always count
on. The downside: *I had someone in my life that I could always count on.*

I never learned until long after my father died how to problem-
solve or weigh the details of a situation and make an independent, well-
informed decision all on my own. I also learned far too late that having
a strong male figure in your immediate sphere does *not* mean he will be
heroic. In fact, those expectations can put a lot of added pressure on a
relationship in the real world—the world where retired Marine Corps
Officer Dad no longer exists and mere mortal men are trying, just like
you, to figure things out for themselves.

I have come to believe that part of the grace that God extends to us includes the lessons we learn through the really tough times. In many cases, He's not going to prevent us from falling into unexpected trouble, but He will be there to walk through it with us. So jumping into something impulsively, even with the best of intentions to help someone, might just be a "trap," as the proverb says—a trap to the sav*er* as well as the sav*ee.*

When no one has been there to pick me up, put me back on my feet, and tell me which way to go in order to find safety, I've had to figure it out. Not always gracefully, and certainly not always without consequence or even regret, but always with a Silent Partner at my side to help me to keep going when strength fails...and to help me learn a valuable lesson.

You know that saying, "Give a man a fish, feed him for a day; teach a man to fish, feed him for a lifetime"? I always thought that was well and good, until it came down to it. I'd much rather order the salmon at my favorite restaurant than have to catch it, clean it, and cook it! But isn't it nice to know that you can if you have to? — Sandie

TODAY'S PRAYER

Lord Jesus, thank You for the hard times where
You've miraculously carried me through. But thank You also
for the times when You've allowed me to learn.

A Pfennig for
Your Thoughts

*Hear, O Israel: The L*ORD* our God, the L*ORD* is one.*
DEUTERONOMY 6:4

The shelf above my computer is filled with photos of my husband, kids, grandkids, and deceased pets (including Keith, the county fair–won goldfish that lived to the ripe old age of 11). And the wall behind the pictures is papered with dozens of old saws, adages, parables, and proverbs.

The two I quote most often are, "Do or do not; there *is* no try" and "Good enough never is." (Just ask my kids!) The message is threefold:

Commitment ignites action; your word is your bond; practice your beliefs consistently.

"Stand for something," I've said a hundred times if I've said it once, "or you'll fall for anything." After speeches like that, my kids had every right to expect that, as their mother, I would set a proper example. Self-confidence, integrity, a willingness to dig in and perform the same jobs I'd asked them to do was, of course, important. But so was supporting them—especially when "slipshod" seemed to be their modus operandi—and giving them a chance to prove that maybe, just maybe, they really *could* find faster, easier, more effective ways of getting things accomplished.

I'm reasonably certain that long before Ferdinand Porsche built his first automobile, *his* mama bounced her fair share of *pfennigs* off his blankets, which no doubt led to his success. (Remember the now-clichéd response he gave the reporter who asked which was his favorite Porsche? "Why, I haven't built it yet!")

And how could I expect my girls to improve in mind, body, and spirit if they didn't see improvements in me too? Seeking a better, easier way of doing things, in my honest opinion, proves personal growth. Equally important? A willingness to take a risk now and then, instead of merely insisting that things get done *my* way.

Motivating our kids to do the right thing isn't easy, particularly when we're asking them to perform difficult or boring tasks. But as Epicurus taught his young'uns way back when, "A captain earns his reputation during storms." We all want smooth-sailing in our children's future, so why not test their navigation skills while they're still in the boat with us, rather than let them flounder all alone on life's turbulent seas?

Our Father promised always to be there, lifeline at the ready, any time we need Him. If we add "faith in Him" to the lessons we teach our children, they'll have the strength to stand up against those who'd try to steer them off course. If they learn to rely on God with every cell He set pulsing inside them, they'll recognize the grace that can be theirs just by asking for it.

And you know, I can't think of any greater gift to give them than that! ⁓ Loree

TODAY'S PRAYER

To You, Father, belongs eternal praise.
Grace me with understanding so that my words
and actions will bring glory to Your most holy name.
Bless me with the wisdom and knowledge I'll need
to teach these things to my children, who will
teach their children, so that Your loving grace
will beat in their hearts down through the generations
until we gather together with You in paradise.

Just Kidding!

Like a maniac shooting flaming arrows of death is one
who deceives their neighbor and says, "I was only joking!"
PROVERBS 26:18–19

Recently, I watched another news story about a child who was bullied to the point of attempting suicide. When I see such things, I want to cradle the poor victim in my arms and hug him up. I also want to grab hold of the bullies and throttle them.

I was never the victim of bullying as a child, other than the occasional mean girl who muttered insults under her breath. I never suffered at the hands of a group of kids, which can even take the shape of just one bully and a roomful of silent bystanders.

I'm glad celebrities have taken up the cause of the underdog. There have been anti-bullying movements in the past in the schools and on the news, but what I've seen lately has been focused on the victims, with emphatic assurance that life gets better. And messages of conviction urge bystanders to step in to defend victims whenever they can.

That can be a scary thing to do. I remember, as a painfully shy little girl, riding the school bus and seeing a pushy girl make a big show of pretending she was in love with the heavyset boy across the aisle. She did it strictly to make fun of him. How absurd, her joke insinuated, that she would ever consider falling for someone like him. And I just sat there, staring at the ground, afraid to step in and defend him. The shame of remaining silent still burns today.

But there's another kind of bullying that's far less obvious and in many ways more devious. I've experienced it, and I've seen it between Christian husbands and wives. It's heartbreaking in its unfairness. In front of others, a husband makes a snide comment to his wife about some flaw and she's forced to either "grin and bear it" as if she doesn't care or confront him about the jab. If she does confront him, he chuckles—he might even grab her and give her a cuddle—and he says something like, "I was only joking, honey!" Or a wife might do the same about some perceived shortcoming on her husband's part, only to laugh and claim that he's being overly sensitive if he calls her on it.

That kind of bully hides behind jocularity and pretends that he or she has been misunderstood when confronted by the victim. Bystanders almost *always* notice the tension behind the so-called teasing. How often have you witnessed that kind of attack and felt comfortable to step up to defend the victim? Most of us stare at the ground like that frightened little girl on the bus. Or we smile and hope the moment will pass.

There's a place for grace in these circumstances. God's grace can shield us against words with deceitful motives. And His grace can provide us with words of encouragement for victims of such "joking."

Trish

TODAY'S PRAYER

Dearest Lord, You know the tenor of every person's heart.
Please convict me if I'm ever tempted to shoot one of those
"arrows" at someone. And please help me to don You
as my protection, should one of those arrows ever fly at me.

Dangerous

But grow in the grace and knowledge of our Lord and Savior Jesus Christ. To him be glory both now and forever! Amen.

2 PETER 3:18

Too young. He was too young to die. She was too young to become a widow. Their children were too young to sit in the front row at a funeral, too young to squeeze out a smile and say "Thank you for coming" as the mourners filed past.

Condolences and casseroles sustained them for those first intense, swirling, numb days of grief. Reality followed on the heels of the casseroles and cakes. As it often happens, single parenting was accompanied by financial desperation. She breathed only because she knew she had to and dove into God's Word the way a sobbing child might bury herself in her father's shoulder.

I didn't meet her until years later, long after her path changed again with a corporate job that more than met their financial needs and an outpouring of God's grace that met every cry of their hearts.

Comfortable suburban life settled around their family. Her children graduated, married, and blessed her with grandchildren. And then God spoke.

When she prayed for the Lord to send someone to work with the homeless and destitute in the inner city, He said, "*You* go."

"Me, Lord? I'm about to retire. I don't feel confident driving through the inner city, much less living there. I know what it's like to be poor and hurting, but You brought me out of that. Thanks again, by the way. A silver-haired Caucasian suburban grandmother? I'm the unlikeliest candidate."

Despite the shocked expressions of…well, everyone…she moved

from hard-won comfort to the graffitied heart of one of the poorest neighborhoods in the country, into the heart of danger.

Today she claims she moved out of danger to a place of safety.

"Complacency is dangerous," she says. "I left complacency and took up residence where my heavenly Father is responsible for my safety. I was in danger of growing indifferent because I was comfortable."

Her eyes shine with reflections from the poverty-stricken and spiritually troubled to whom she's shown God's love, those whose lives she's seen transformed by His grace. "I can't be indifferent anymore. I can only live by grace."

Grace applied to the fatherless. Grace lavished on the homeless. Grace poured out for those whose pupils are perpetually dilated from who-knows-what, and whose clothes—both sets—smell rancid with the sludge of life. Grace offered freely with no hope of "You can pay me back later." Grace the way God designed it.

I have a lot of growing to do. ⟿ Cynthia

TODAY'S PRAYER
• •

Lord God, even when my budget is pinched or my patience
with my husband is parchment-thin or what's on the plate
in front of me isn't as appetizing as it seemed when I first
saw it on the Food Channel, my life is far more comfortable
than those whose lives are endangered when they sit
on their front stoops or those who don't worry about
the price of gas because they don't own a car. I too seldom
let my heart break with what breaks Yours. Lord,
what do I know of Your grace? The request comes out
in a stutter when I ask You to t-t-t-teach me.

Critics, Schmitics

He mocks proud mockers but shows favor to the humble and oppressed.
PROVERBS 3:34

I love the way Jesus ignored the critics. So self-assured of his mission, even at a very young age, He traveled the path from manger to cross with enviable laser vision.

In the weeks leading up to the release of a novel, the reviews start to hit the forums. To a large extent, most of the reviewers of my books for the inspirational market have been Christians themselves. Somewhere within the pages of my novels, they've been able to find someone or something with which to identify, so they've warmed up to the characters and their challenges.

Recently, publishers have been hooking up with Amazon to provide free downloads of certain books for Kindle customers. These promotions have the benefit of supporting the relatively new idea of e-books as well as getting the work of various writers into hands they might otherwise never reach.

On the downside, however, people really love getting something for free. Often it doesn't matter in the least whether it's something they would normally purchase—*it's free!* So people who don't gravitate toward romantic fiction, particularly geared for the Christian market, download our books and are surprised by the content. In response, they hurry over to the website and post one-star reviews because they don't like that the author "pushed Jesus" on them or they feel like romance is a waste of text.

But…*it's Christian romantic comedy.* So a little Jesus and a lot of romance is kind of required, isn't it? And now the one-star reviews have pulled all those other four- and five-star ratings out of their happy heights. With those first few bad reviews, I had visions of tracking them down, explaining my point of view and… But, of course, that wouldn't be wise. I worried about those one-stars just the same. They gave me queasy stomachs and pounding headaches, and I started wishing I could put a stop to those free downloads altogether.

Cut to: Sandie, growing up.

There are always going to be critics. There will be people who genuinely don't appreciate my writing alongside haters who simply don't like overweight, sarcastic redheads with the arrogance to believe that God has called them to do something in life. I get that. In fact, I'm annoyed by myself all the time.

Proverbs 4:25–27 admonishes us to keep our eyes fixed on the road ahead without swerving to the right or the left. I think that's the secret. Don't get pulled into battles you can't win; they will drain your energy in their futility. Just press on, staying humble about the mission God has given you; maintain your focus and don't get distracted by the haters (or the one-star givers). As today's verse promises, He will provide the grace needed to carry you through. In the bigger picture, isn't that really all you need? ⁓ Sandie

TODAY'S PRAYER

Lord, help me to keep my eyes on You, no matter what
comes at me from the right or the left. Let me focus
on honoring You in all I do without thoughts
and efforts directed at pleasing people instead.
Thank You for setting my course and preparing my future
in spite of the bumps and obstacles.

Step Away
from the Sack!

Return to the LORD your God, for he is gracious and compassionate,
slow to anger and abounding in love.

JOEL 2:13

Okay. All right. So I get it: we all get mad from time to time. It's normal. In some cases, it's healthy. At the very least, it's *human.* Why, even Jesus lost His temper in the temple.

And therein lies the rub: if you're gonna go ballistic, you'd best have a justifiable reason. If only the <ahem> gentleman ahead of me at the airport last week had lived by those words.

There are rules posted here and there in the airport—not many, but since they change like the weather, everybody knows it's mostly monkey-see-monkey-do once you enter the terminal:

Check in at the ticket counter (even if you've done so online) and release your suitcase to the agent. Put your ID and boarding pass where they're easy to get to, and when you reach the security lanes, remove your shoes, coat, metal-buckled belt, bracelet, watch, and whatever else might go *beep* in the X-ray tunnel.

Empty your pockets of coins, phone, throat lozenges, and tissues—even used ones—then open your briefcase and purse and place them, with your laptop and everything else listed above, into an ugly gray plastic bin. Now wait your turn at shoving the works down the conveyor belt, and then wait your turn *again* as the guards randomly select which passengers will walk through the metal detector and which they'll put into the we-can-see-all-of-you-and-we-do-mean-*all*-of-you booth.

I'm sure you've watched old Westerns where cattle are herded into a corral. Take your behavioral cues from the bovines, my friends, and just moo–o–ove quietly along, because trying to buck the system will only clog the chute. And nobody wants that, because on The Other Side…freedom, wonderful freedom awaits!

So anyway, although this so-called seasoned traveler-guy in front of me knew all of this, he *still* blew a gasket when a guard said he had to dispose of his fast-food sack. Mr. Not-so-Cool waved his arms. Stomped his blue-socked feet. Hollered and cursed and made hit-and-miss threats until he was hoarse and his face went purple and sweaty.

Was he justified, losing his temper? Mmm…nah.

Did anyone in the line show pity? Mmm…yeah, but his red-faced wife wasn't among them.

Safe on The Other Side, I prayed for the guy whose conduct made me wonder if he had a relationship with God. I prayed that if he didn't, he'd *find* God, and soon, so that he could learn firsthand what it's like to be loved by a being who is slow to anger, gracious and compassionate, abounding in love…even when the behavior of His children tempts *Him* to go ballistic.

I prayed for the rest of the people in line, too, and for the flight crew and myself. Because, let's face it, there but by the grace of God…

Loree

TODAY'S PRAYER

Father of all, I pray that You will plant the seeds of tranquillity
and harmony in my heart, so that no matter where I go,
no matter what I do, Your grace will guide my words
and actions and make me a true instrument of Your peace.

Christian Is
as Christian Does

You, however, must teach what is appropriate to sound doctrine.

TITUS 2:1

Not too long ago, I wrote an e-mail to my daughter about a family member with whom I was frustrated. It was angry. It was even snarky. My daughter was a safe person to vent to because she and I both love this family member and nothing I said in frustration would shake that love. I just needed to blow off steam.

The only problem was that, in my emotional distraction, I didn't enter my daughter's e-mail address. I entered the family member's address—the one about whom I was rudely complaining—and pushed SEND.

I didn't discover my mistake for hours, and I nearly went into shock when I did. I think the only time I've sweated more was when I was in labor with my kids.

Never has an apology—a profuse apology, I should add—come easier. It killed me that I had inflicted such hurt on a loved one. I'm blessed that she has such a forgiving spirit.

The memory of my embarrassing error arose when I looked into today's verse. I had always thought that "sound doctrine" meant sensible, reasonable, well-substantiated doctrine. So it sounds as if the verse means "make sure what you teach is biblically based." Certainly that's always true. But apparently, for purposes of this verse, the meaning is that we must teach doctrine that conforms to the Lord's Word and results in encouraging Christlike behavior.

Certainly we see that quality in the teaching we receive on Sunday morning from our pastor, who wants his words to motivate us to live as Christ wants us to. And Sunday school teachers have that result in mind when they find creative ways to instill God's tenets in the hearts of our little ones. Our Bible-study groups are all about an end result that includes behavior so attractive that others will be drawn to what we have in our hearts. We should mirror Christ in our attractive behavior.

Ahem.

I think it's safe to say that my behavior—my nasty, ranting little e-mail—didn't exactly fall within the parameters of "sound doctrine." Because, when you think about it, if we profess to be followers of Christ, our actions and words teach the world about how Christ affects lives and choices. What we do is a picture of what we are. And what I was at that moment wasn't just distracted. It was mean and horribly hurtful. I'm sure I didn't just break my loved one's heart. I know I broke my own. And I surely broke His. Look at me! I'm the good little Christian, and look how I show it! Yeesh.

As beaten to death as the phrase is, "What Would Jesus Do" is still a smart thought to review before taking emotional action. If Jesus had had access to e-mail, something tells me that He would have written something my loved one would have absolutely cherished. ⟶ Trish

TODAY'S PRAYER
. . . .

Sweet Lord Jesus, You're such an amazing role model,
and Your perfection is an impossible goal we all strive for.
Please help me to stop and think about how my behavior
represents You, especially before I do or say anything
in the spirit of frustration or anger. I love You.

Trying Not to Limp

*Like a broken tooth or a lame foot is reliance
on the unfaithful in a time of trouble.*

PROVERBS 25:19

I'm way too young to need a knee replacement. Waaaaaay too young. Decades too young. But along with crooked teeth and stick-straight hair that actually resists even industrial-strength curling irons, my siblings and I inherited bad right knees. One sister got her knee replacement a few years ago, brave woman. The rest of us are lined up like Marine recruits waiting to get our heads shaved. Or knees, rather.

I blame it on the jump rope. Not the jump roping I did as a kid, but that resurgence of interest a couple of years ago when I thought jumping rope on my deck was a better idea than other forms of Dread Exercise. It wasn't pretty, but it elevated my heart rate more than leaning across my desk to grab a reference book.

Apparently my knees were just waiting for a reason to go on strike. The paint on their picket signs had dried long ago. They awaited the call: *She's gone and done it. Spread the word. She's jumping rope.*

My current schedule won't accommodate knee surgery and months of rehab until three cycles of leap years have come and gone. So I'm coping. And trying not to limp.

Well-practiced now, I can sometimes pull off a nearly normal gait, although it takes concentration and the use of muscles designed for other purposes. There's a downside to walking without a limp. It sometimes lulls me into thinking my knee is reliable.

I'm not a farm-tractor kind of person, but once in a while my husband the hobby farmer needs a hired hand to help him with a project that involves someone to run the levers and whatever those other knobs are on a tractor.

"Just climb on up there, honey, and lower the bucket while I slide this metal plate under it."

The blankest of stares washes over me. So Bill tries a new tactic. "Lower the bucket. The lever to the right of the steering wheel."

Still blank.

"Steering wheel. The round thing."

I know what a steering wheel is. I was stopped by, "Climb on up there." It's not so easy with a bum knee. It's either the good one or the bad one that has to go first for a successful climb. I can never remember which one until after I've tried it. Climbing down from the tractor is worse. I can't be sure my knee will hold me.

That's the truth that tops my list of blessings today. Not that my knee can't be counted on, but that the Lord always can. I never have to wonder if His love is going to give out, if I'm putting too much pressure on His patience, if leaning that hard on His grace will make it collapse and send me tumbling awkwardly to the ground. He is always and ever reliable.

No matter how hard I work not to limp, the fragility of my knee remains. But I never have to wonder if His grace can hold me.

⌒ Cynthia

TODAY'S PRAYER
. . . .

Thank You, Lord, ever faithful One, for promising
and delivering unfailing strength I can count on.
Reliable, dependable, faithful God, I worship You.

God Always
Plans Ahead

"So there is hope for your descendants," declares the Lord.

JEREMIAH 31:17

I didn't even know we had armadillos in Florida! They were all over the place in Texas, but the humid, hurricane-ridden peninsula of Florida just never struck me as a habitat for animals that have to wear armor 24/7. But just like God, whether you believe or not, they're here!

There are many qualities about these creatures that I have come to despise.

They are obnoxious. Even when caught in the act of digging a hole in one's yard, they ignore shouts, threats, even soda cans hurled in frustration that just bounce right off their backs.

They come out at two or three in the morning, to the great torment and frustration of dogs living inside. Consequently, home owners are ripped from a sound sleep almost every night by their furious, barking dog.

They're completely indiscriminate adversaries. They dig holes everywhere. Like near the side of the driveway by the car so you lose your footing; next to the garage, until they reach the foundation—then they keep right on digging; under the fence so that the dog thinks she stands a chance of fitting beneath it…and ultimately gets stuck.

One recent afternoon, my dog, Sophie, started barking and snarling at the sliding door to the backyard, and I immediately began searching for the culprit. Instead of an armadillo, my eyes landed on a baby bird and its mother chirping wildly from atop the fence, cheering on her baby as it hopped and flapped in an effort to take flight. Closer examination revealed a nest in the tree branches above the bird, and I realized Baby had fallen from it, unable to fly beyond the confines of my backyard.

To my absolute horror, a huge black crow swooped in out of nowhere and went after the little bird. Mama and I both sprang into action to shoo the crow away. It took several attempts to deter the big bully, and while I shook my fist at it, Mama did something completely unexpected by nudging her baby toward the fence until it fell into a shallow hole left by…an armadillo!

While Baby stayed in that hole, Mama flew up to the nest, presumably to look after her other little ones. Once the coast was definitely clear and the black crow had flown off in pursuit of easier prey, the mother bird hopped down to encourage her offspring to come out from its hiding place and try once again to fly over the fence.

I couldn't help marveling over the fact that the damages done by my greatest nemesis in recent memory had actually provided much-needed shelter in time of crisis. If not for that messy hole under my fence, that baby bird might not have escaped.

Isn't that just like God? He so often casts the net beneath our high-wire act long before we ever realize we're going to fall. Those things which are meant for our harm, God has already fully understood, and He has set our escape into place ahead of time. ⟶ Sandie

TODAY'S PRAYER

Lord Jesus, I am humbled by Your ability to answer
my prayers before I've even finished praying them.
You are truly awesome!

Out with the Old, In with the New

*"The Lord bless and keep you; the Lord make his face
shine on you and be gracious to you;
the Lord turn his face toward you and give you peace."*

NUMBERS 6:24-26

Don't you just love those ads that come tucked into your Sunday paper? You know, the ones that promise that you can walk into a store and leave with just about anything, from a wide-screen television to a top-of-the-line computer...and not pay a penny *for two whole years*! What we *don't* love is the way that big fat payment due sneaks up and bites us once the twenty-four months are up.

This past Christmas, my husband and I made a pact: we'd trade our clunky old television set for one of those jazzy new wide-screen versions, and because it wasn't inexpensive, the TV would serve as birthday, anniversary, Mother's, and Fathers' Day gifts throughout the year. And we'd make regular payments, y'know, to spare ourselves the whole ugly "outrun the payment monster" scene.

We've enjoyed the dickens out of the TV. Writing those checks every month? Not so much. But the whole buy-now, pay-later process got me to thinking about how many other old things we've traded for new. Hundreds, I'd guess, over the course of our decades-long marriage. And *that* got me to thinking about how God gave us the Old Testament after the New one.

I made the mistake of bringing this up at Bible study. I say "mistake" because oh, what a noise it started! "The Old Testament is 'all law,'" said one guy, "and the New Testament is 'all grace!'" His wife agreed—*loudly.* "The Old Testament God was harsh and unforgiving. But He softened up when He became a Father."

"Do you realize," I asked, "that there are at least twenty references to grace in the Old Testament?"

Husband: "But it didn't *mean* the same thing."

Wife: "Right! It meant *favor.*"

Semantics? I didn't think so then. I don't think so now. But <shrug> to each his own Bible, right?

Wrong! Noah found grace at the Bible's start (Genesis 6:8), and Esther got some too (Esther 2:17). Grace and glory are found in Psalm 84:11 (NKJV), and the Messianic king was filled with grace in Psalm 45:2. And if the Twenty-Third Psalm isn't 100 percent grace, I don't know what is!

I'm sure our heavenly Father saw this mini-debate eons before that Bible study meeting had even been scheduled, and because it's a microscopic example of how Christians would convince themselves that they could walk out of life by paying for their sins with good deeds and prayers, He rewrote the old laws…and replaced them with one brandnew, easy-to-understand rule: thanks to the sacrifice of God's only Son, we can walk out of life and into paradise because *Jesus* paid for our sins. And we'll never experience that scary, "The bill is due; pay up!" feeling again. ⌁ Loree

TODAY'S PRAYER

O Lord Jesus, how I love You! I thank You too,
for not only did You give me a ticket to paradise,
but You paid for it with Your suffering and Your blood.
I am unworthy of Your loving sacrifice
and humbled by Your love for me.

Gotta Stay Sharp!

As iron sharpens iron, so one person sharpens another.
PROVERBS 27:17

Writing is a solitary profession. Typically an author spends a good part of her day on her own, sitting before a computer. And if she's a novelist, she mostly interacts with people who exist only in her imagination.

I'm a novelist, and I'm also single, *and* I'm an empty nester. These three facets of my current life weren't always so, but they've all settled in at once and I expect this relative "aloneness" to be the case for the foreseeable future.

And I couldn't be more thrilled.

Don't get me wrong. I thoroughly loved raising my kids and having them running around me in all stages of their formative years. They were—and still are—the best part of my life. Moving into the grandparenting stage of childrearing has been yet another blessing, but that's an entirely different, less-demanding situation altogether.

And I don't regret having been married, despite the sad path my marriage took. I know myself well. Had I not gone through the experience, I would always wonder what I had missed, and I wouldn't have so many of the fantastic people in my life that I do today.

But I absolutely love my alone time. Always have. There's something to be said for reaching a stage in life when you can call your own shots without stepping on anyone else's schedule, needs, or toes.

Still. Today's verse provides such a valid comment that I know I need to take it to heart. When you live alone, it can become very easy to let your involvement with other people take too low a position on the to-do list. Not good. The concept of relationship is so important that God is *three persons!* There's no denying His intention for us to be relational creatures.

Not only do we need others for the joy of friendship, love, and fun, but we need each other to stay sharp. As a writer, I make a point of passing everything I write before my critique partners, because I miss so much otherwise. I don't notice where I've made mistakes in form or logic or where I could have made something better. Our lives, and especially our faith, need the same kind of sharpening.

I need to be a part of a church body in order to hear good teaching on His Word rather than simply lean on my own interpretation. I need to spend time in friendship with other Christian women so I grow and remain empathetic to others rather than focus on my own wishes, needs, and struggles. I have things to contribute to the lives of others as well. God didn't design me and give me whatever gifts I have just to have me hide them under a bushel (or in front of a computer).

— Trish

TODAY'S PRAYER

Dear God, You've been so gracious in my life, blessing me with the love and interaction of many beautiful, wonderful people. I thank You that You have also blessed me with both peace and joy during this more solitary season of my life. I ask that You keep me always motivated to enjoy the pleasure of friends, family, and fellow believers in order to remain sharp in my devotion to You and Your plan.

Sew Blessed

*"We do not make requests of you because we are righteous,
but because of your great mercy. Lord, listen! Lord, forgive!
Lord, hear and act! For your sake, my God, do not delay,
because your city and your people bear your Name."*

DANIEL 9:18–19

New friends might find it curious or even a bit disturbing that I used to sew my family's clothes. I still have pictures of the matching calico granny dresses I made for my daughter and me. If she'd been older than three at the time, she might have objected more strenuously.

What was my first sewing project? I don't remember. That might be a merciful memory loss. I bonded with a sewing machine in fifth grade. Some projects turned out admirably. If I hadn't sewn the sleeves in backward, the kelly-green wool dress I made for 4-H could have warranted at least an honorable-mention ribbon.

After years of practice with patterns and pins and whatever fabric was on sale, I made my own wedding dress, my bridesmaids' dresses, and the miniature version for the flower girl. Long, flowing sleeves were "in" back in 1972. Who knew it would be 100 degrees with 4000 percent humidity on our wedding day? I'm not sure my bridesmaids are ready to forgive me yet.

Budget-conscious by necessity, as a newlywed I also tried my hand at sewing clothes for my husband. The results hovered between unnerving and disturbing. Wouldn't you be unnerved by the idea of a homemade sky-blue polyester leisure suit? If I ever wonder whether my husband is a good sport, I think of that fashionless statement and swallow my wondering.

Did I mention that I attached the sleeves of my wedding dress backward too? I ripped them out and reattached them the correct way before the wedding. No one knew they'd been sewn twice.

"You made your own wedding gown?"

"I did. Not flawlessly, but…"

It occurs to me that no matter how hard I try or how practiced I am, my best righteousness is sleeves-sewn-in-backward.

I don't pray because I deserve God's attention, but because He offers it. I love Him because He first loved me (1 John 4:19). I don't follow Jesus because I was bright enough to realize that was a smart move, but because He said, "Come. Follow Me."

"Not because of righteous things we had done, but because of his mercy. He saved us." Same message in the New Testament book of Titus (3:5) as in the Old Testament book of Daniel. Sounds like a theme, doesn't it?

The Lord responds not because I frame my prayer perfectly—oh, the pressure!—but because I belong to Him. I bear His Name.

How freeing!

What do I deserve? If I didn't have this propensity for sewing sleeves in backward, maybe honorable mention. What am I offered? Everything.

Sewing update: These days I'd rather stitch words together than French-seam a silk shirt, which, for the record, is not as hard as it sounds. Making a French seam, that is. ⟶ Cynthia

TODAY'S PRAYER

. . . .

Father God, You who deserves my all, backward as it often
is, I'm in awe of Your willingness to keep loving me,
keep steering me, keep hearing me,
keep letting me bear Your Name.

Bottles (and Bottles!) of Tears

Record my misery; list my tears on your
scroll—are they not in your record?

PSALM 56:8

I love this Scripture! It's one of the first verses that really grabbed me and stuck with me when I started studying the Word. The translation I read at the time said, "You number my wanderings; put my tears into Your bottle" (NKJV). Oh, how I love that picture!

A college friend once told me she thought I wasted a lot of energy by "allowing myself" to be such an emotional person. "All the tears and inner turmoil could be energy so much better spent!" she exclaimed. I remember laughing instead of responding, wondering how one simply *decides* not to cry when their feelings have been hurt or they've been disappointed. For me, it's never been a matter of turning the water-works on or off; it's more of an involuntary response, like sneezing.

I cry at a Hallmark commercial or a movie trailer, so you can imagine how many tears fall at a personal injustice or a misunderstanding with a friend. The idea that Jesus pays such close attention to what's going on with me that He collects them, keeps an audit, or saves them up in a bottle on His office shelf is one that paints the picture that I am *cherished*. I am so *valuable* to Him that He keeps track of my tears!

I think we Christians spend a lot of time talking and thinking and praying about how wondrous God is. We praise Him for His greatness, His omnipotence, His overwhelming glory. He's huge and powerful, and nothing is impossible for Him. As the great Rich Mullins taught us, "Our God is an awesome God! He reigns from heaven above!"

Shew! It's staggering, isn't it?

But what of the sweet, intimate love He has for us? That's a little more difficult to comprehend at times, right? After all, we're so unworthy, so faithless.

When my marriage was falling apart, I went to stay with my parents for a couple of weeks while I decided what to do. One night, my husband called the house to speak to me, and I heard my mother say, "No, I don't hate you. But you have to understand that my daughter has cried herself to sleep over you six out of eight nights in a row, so that's going to impact me."

Although my relationship with her was somewhat strained during that time, I remember taking a step back from what stood between us when I heard that phone conversation. My mom had kept track of the tears I'd shed, and on a much smaller scale than the great God of all keeping an account of my heartaches!

Grace allows us to share intimacy with our Father in the shadow of His greatness. And today's Scripture reminds us of that glorious dichotomy. It tells us that He cares so deeply about us that He keeps track of our misery and pain. Every tear shed is counted, like the hairs on our head are numbered. How cool is that? ⸺ Sandie

TODAY'S PRAYER

Lord, help me to remember that You are watching,
that You are feeling my pain. And help me to remember
also that, when I make someone else cry,
You're watching that as well.

The Great Round Tuit

"Thus, by their fruit you will recognize them."
MATTHEW 7:20

I took one of those silly online quizzes this morning, titled "Are You a Procrastinator?" I'll share my score…later.

For now, if I hope to avoid procrastination, I guess I'd better figure out what it *is*.

The first example of procrastination that comes to mind is Scarlett O'Hara, with her "I'll worry about that tomorrow" mantra. Remember how, as the movie begins, she's *working* toward arriving late to her neighbors' fancy shindig…because she was afraid that without the grand entrance, Ashley wouldn't notice her?

According to today's psychiatrists, that very type of fear causes more procrastination than anything else. We can't fail at something if we never get around to it, right?

The pros also say that procrastinators are made, not born. Which means that if we grew up watching our mothers and fathers trying to avoid getting things done, it's a pretty sure bet we'll walk that slow mile in their shoes.

We can blame distraction for our procrastination too.

And while we're at it, let's add perfectionism to the list, because, hey, it takes a lot of time to dot every *i* and cross every *t*!

Experts also claim that most of us don't take procrastination seriously enough. A little "there but by the grace of God," maybe?

If so, I'm in good company, since 20 percent of Americans call themselves procrastinators. We're late paying bills. Late to work. Late in sending birthday cards. Unfortunately, that's when procrastination leads to prevarication. Can't just waltz in late for Thanksgiving dinner without a believable *lie* to explain things, now can we?

Now about my score: 32 out of 100 (the higher the number, the bigger the procrastinator) means I'm not much of a putter-offer after all. I have a feeling that if the good Lord had graded the test, He'd quickly point out that procrastination can be a major setback to my reaching the goals He has set for me. And He'd probably say that, with a score of 32, I have plenty of room for improvement. Because seriously? If I'm all wrapped up in finding ways to get *out* of doing His will, how will anyone recognize me as a child of God?

Which reminds me of the time when my eldest daughter was about three and she colored a picture of the family: Dad, Mom, herself, and little sister, the cat and dog…and a big round ball, smack in the middle, that she'd colored black.

"What's that?" I asked as I taped the drawing to the fridge.

"Why, a round tuit, of course."

"But…what's a round tuit?"

"It's what you and daddy say *all the time*."

And then I remembered the dozens of times my husband and I had said, "Not now, sweetie, but we'll get around to it soon, okay?"

Procrastination comes in many shapes and forms, and sometimes it comes in rainbow colors too. ⟶ Loree

TODAY'S PRAYER

I humbly thank You, Lord, for providing Your Word,
for in it I find peace and comfort, answers and reassurance,
and the strength of soul to do what You have led me to do,
so that I will always reflect the bright light
of Your love into this sometimes dark world.

This One Is for Keeps

And so after waiting patiently,
Abraham received what was promised.

HEBREWS 6:15

When my son was in grade school I was big on volunteering with any school- or church-sponsored activity in which he participated. I hadn't been able to stay at home from work when my daughter was little, so I wanted to take advantage of the opportunity to be a more obvious presence in my boy's life while I could.

So it was I found myself herding a large number of fifth graders during a breakout session at Vacation Bible School. All week the kids had been taking part in crafts that spelled out something wonderful about Jesus and salvation. Every morning my group and a couple hundred other kids enjoyed raucous, funny, uplifting songs about the Lord. Even the obstacle-course-type activities held some kind of symbolism about God and the redemptive sacrifice of His beloved Son.

It was salvation, all morning, every morning, for five days. And now, as we neared the end of the week, we teachers were afforded the opportunity to simply talk with our charges and see if they had any questions or had the desire to turn their hearts over to the Lord.

Since I had the oldest group—and since most of them had been attending my church since infancy—there weren't many kids in the group who hadn't already taken that big step into eternity. My job was simple.

But I felt a little tweaking in my mind and asked the group, "Are there any of you who worry about losing your salvation?"

I was floored by the number of hands that went up. It broke my heart.

Maybe it had something to do with the fact that sometimes parents' well-meaning promises end up broken for one unfortunate reason or another. Maybe it was because of the unfathomable nature of salvation and how Christ's sacrifice makes it possible; perhaps that's hard for kids to fully grasp. Or maybe those kids who raised their hands simply hadn't been assured enough that God doesn't break His promises, that by His nature He is *unable* to break His promises.

The "patient waiting" in today's verse refers to the twenty-five-plus years Abraham waited for a son after God promised him he would have one. Yes, Abraham slipped in his patience, which resulted in Ishmael's birth. Still, God's promise was fulfilled.

God's promises are forever. None of us means to lie by breaking our promises, but that's essentially what we do. God doesn't lie. He can't.

I assured those kids that their salvation was there to stay. God had made a promise to them—to all of us—that, if we made the decision to accept salvation as a free gift from Christ, we would *never* lose that salvation. "We're saved," I told them, "not because of what we do, but because of what He did. And that's a promise that will never change."
— Trish

TODAY'S PRAYER

. . . .

Heavenly Lord, Your abundant grace knows no bounds.
Certainly there is nothing I can do to destroy that grace
and cause You to withdraw the promise of salvation
You made to me. I will always strive to honor that promise,
that gift, but I will also embrace the fact
that You made a promise that will not fail.

Mercy's Law

He saved us, not because of righteous things we had done,
but because of his mercy.

TITUS 3:5

For a woman who can count good hair days on one hand...in a mitten...it was a glorious moment. I hadn't made it from the church entrance to the inner doors of the sanctuary before three people stopped me to say, "Hey! I like your hair!"

I looked over my shoulder, but what do you know? They were talking to me.

"Thank you."

"I like the highlights."

Me too. A little adventuresome, maybe. But the carefully placed triangle of ripened-wheat highlights against the burnt caramel underlayers made me feel perky. Besides, the technique camouflaged the encroaching gray.

When the fourth person stopped me to comment on the new 'do, my husband rolled his eyes. He what? That's right. He rolled his eyes. The person who'd complimented my hair said to him, "You don't like it?"

No doubt suffering from some undiscovered medical condition that made him lose all sense of propriety and both of the fragile romantic cells he'd retained throughout our marriage, my husband looked at the wheat triangle and then at the commenter and said, "I keep expecting to see 101 dalmatians coming around the corner."

If I could have captured the looks on the faces of the bystanders...

Cruella de Vil? He thought my hair looked like an evil villainess's?

"Aw, honey. You say the sweetest things!"

That wasn't my reaction. If I remember correctly, I asked our pastor if that morning's sermon happened to be on marriage.

Days earlier, I'd spoken to a MOPS (Mothers of Preschoolers) group. My topic? "Mercy's Laws of Marriage." If Murphy's Law says anything that can go wrong will go wrong, Murphy's Laws of Marriage are similar. The only shirt your husband wants to wear on Sunday is the one that isn't ironed. Only if company is minutes away will your husband want to tackle the plumbing project that's been on his to-do list since the Reagan administration. The potential for forgetfulness is in direct proportion to the event's importance.

My point that day was that as certain as I was of Murphy's Laws of Marriage, I wish I'd known earlier about Mercy's Laws of Marriage—that in God's way of looking at things (including me), mercy gets the last word.

So, as I sat in church beside the man who'd just compared my new hairdo to the coiffure of one of the most disliked women in the world of animation, a woman who hated puppies, I considered my options.

Find a metaphor to describe his cactus-needle beard.

Refuse to talk to my husband for the rest of the day.

Forget he said anything. Show him the kind of mercy the Lord shows me when I do or say something incredibly insensitive and not even a little bit funny.

As the worship music faded and Pastor adjusted his headset microphone, I made my decision. I'd forgive my husband before he asked me to.

Almost as startling as that swipe of wheat across my burnt caramel hair. ⌐ Cynthia

TODAY'S PRAYER

Lord God, it shouldn't be so surprising when I act like You.
It should be the rule rather than the exception.
When I face a Murphy's Law moment today,
please help mercy to get the last word.

Sandra D. Bricker

SANDRA D. BRICKER was an entertainment publicist in Los Angeles for more than fifteen years before becoming a best-selling, award-winning author of laugh-out-loud fiction from the Tampa, Florida, area. As an ovarian cancer survivor, she used her time and effort toward raising awareness and funds for diagnostics and a cure. Her favorite coffee was crème brulee with a shot of sugar-free vanilla cream. Sandie was called home to her heavenly Father in late 2016.

Loree Lough

Once upon a time, Loree Lough sang for her supper. That space reserved in pubs for "the piano lady?" Well, that's where she sat, strumming her Yamaha in cities all over the U.S. and Canada. Now and then, she blows the dust from the old 6-string to croon a tune or two, but mostly, she writes. And with the release of the 3rd book in her third series for Harlequin Heartwarming, "By Way of the Lighthouse," she'll have 111 books on the shelves. She feels blessed that, over the years, most of her stories have earned 4- and 5-star reviews, but what Loree is most proud of are the dozens "Readers' Choice" awards she has won, because it's the readers' opinions she cares most about!

Loree and her husband live in a modest home in Maryland and enjoy spending time at their cozy cabin in Pennsylvania's Allegheny Mountains (where she has nearly perfected her "identify the critter tracks" skills). They have two lovely daughters and seven "grandorables," and because she believes in giving back, Loree donates a portion of her annual income to several worthwhile charities. (See the full list on the "Giving Back" page at http://www.loreelough.com.)

While you're there, Loree hopes you'll drop her a note, because she loves hearing from her readers, some of whom have become lifelong friends! (You can also interact with her at Facebook, Twitter, or Pinterest.)

Trish Perry

Award-winning novelist Trish Perry has written twelve inspirational romances for Harvest House Publishers, Summerside Press, Barbour Publishing, Forget-Me-Not Romances, and Mountain Brook Ink, and she has co-authored three devotionals for Summerside and one for Broadstreet Publishing. She has served as a columnist and as a newsletter editor over the years, as well as a 1980s stockbroker and a board member of the Capital Christian Writers organization in Washington, D.C. She holds a degree in Psychology.

Since the 2006 release of her first novel, *The Guy I'm Not Dating*, Trish has woven romance, humor, friendship, and faith throughout her stories of people seeking fulfilling lives together—and in spite of one another. She loves to entertain readers while exploring how even the faultiest of characters can grow, especially when they get out of God's way. That growth is sometimes frustrating, sometimes poignant, and often hilarious. This theme colors all of Trish's books.

In Love and War (2016) features Trish's latest contemporary romance novella, *More Than Meets the Eye*. She invites you to visit her at www.trishperry.com

Cynthia Ruchti

Cynthia Ruchti tells stories *hemmed in hope* through her award-winning novels, novellas, devotionals, nonfiction, and through speaking events for women and writers. Her books have been recognized—both fiction and nonfiction—by industry honors such as the Selah Awards, Christian Retailing's BEST Awards, AWSA Golden Scrolls, Inspirational Readers' Choice Award, Foreword Book Reviews, IndieFab Book of the Year honors, RT Reviewers' Choice honors, a Christy final, and two Carol Award nominations, among others. She and her husband live in the heart of Wisconsin among forests, cranberry bogs, corn fields, and dairy farms, not far from their three children and five grandchildren. Cynthia is a frequent speaker for women's retreats and writers' conferences, and serves as ACFW's Professional Relations Liaison. Cynthia's books and devotions are inspired by her observations of the intersection of God's story and our stories. No matter the crisis we face, or the grace we need, we can find hope tucked among the truths God laid out for us in His Word. She prays that when readers finish one of her books or attendees hear the last word of a presentation, they'll find renewed courage to say, "I can't unravel. I'm hemmed in hope."

IF YOU ENJOYED THIS BOOK, WILL YOU CONSIDER SHARING THE MESSAGE WITH OTHERS?

Mention the book in a blog post or through Facebook, Twitter, Pinterest, or upload a picture through Instagram.

Recommend this book to those in your small group, book club, workplace, and classes.

Head over to facebook.com/worthypublishing, "LIKE" the page, and post a comment as to what you enjoyed the most.

Tweet "I recommend reading #GraceIsLikeChocolate by @worthypub"

Pick up a copy for someone you know who would be challenged and encouraged by this message.

Write a book review online.

Visit us at worthypublishing.com

 twitter.com/worthypub

 worthypub.tumblr.com

 facebook.com/worthypublishing

 pinterest.com/worthypub

 instagram.com/worthypub

 youtube.com/worthypublishing